Teachings
of the
Buddha

Teachings of the Buddha

The Wisdom of the Dharma,
from the Pali Canon
to the Sutras

Desmond Biddulph
and Darcy Flynn

Photographs by
John Cleare

SHELTER HARBOR PRESS
NEW YORK

Teachings of the Buddha
Desmond Biddulph and Darcy Flynn

This 2016 edition printed for Shelter Harbor Press by arrangement with EMEX LTD

Shelter Harbor Press
603 West 115th Street, Suite 163
New York, NY 10025

For sales, please contact:
info@shelterharborpress.com

Copyright © Watkins Media 2009
Text copyright © Watkins Media 2009
Photography copyright © John Cleare 2009

The right of Desmond Biddulph and Darcy Flynn to be identified as the Authors of this text has been asserted in accordance with the Copyright, Designs and Patents Act of 1988.

All rights reserved. No part of this book may be reproduced in any form or by any electronic or mechanical means, including information storage and retrieval systems, without permission in writing from the publisher, except by a reviewer who may quote brief passages in a review.

Managing Editor: Christopher Westhorp
Managing Designer: Clare Thorpe
Picture Editor: Julia Brown

ISBN: 978-1-62795-047-3

10 9 8 7 6 5 4 3 2 1

Typeset in Present and Skia
Colour reproduction by Colourscan,
 Singapore
Printed and bound in China by Imago

Notes:
The terminology used is generally
Sanskrit (S.), with the Pali (P.) form added
or occasionally used instead where appropriate.

Abbreviations used throughout this book:
CE Common Era (the equivalent of AD)
BCE Before the Common Era (the equivalent
 of BC)
b. born, d. died, r. reigned.

Contents

Introduction ... 6

The Teachings ... 40

    The Twelve-Linked Chain of Causation ... 42

    The Three Signs of Being ... 62

    The Three Fires ... 78

    The Middle Path ... 90

    The Four Noble Truths ... 96

    The Noble Eightfold Path ... 106

    The *Paramitas* ... 114

    Cultivation of the Heart ... 132

    Mindfulness ... 140

    Meditation ... 160

Index ... 174

Further reading ... 176

About the authors/photographer ... 176

Introduction

There are about 350 million Buddhists worldwide, making it the fourth largest of the world's traditional religions. At one time, Europeans classified Buddhism as a philosophy rather than a religion, something to be read and reflected upon instead of practised. Just as Christians today follow the teachings of Jesus, a man who lived some 2,000 years ago, the adherents of Buddhism follow in the footsteps of a sage, who was born Prince Siddhartha Gautama more than 2,500 years ago in the foothills of the mighty Himalayas, which stretch from the burning plains of India through modern-day Nepal up onto the high-altitude Tibetan plateau, the "roof of the world".

The Buddha, as Prince Siddhartha became known, developed teachings and practices as a result of his disturbing observations on the fleeting nature of this life, which culminated in a final insight that resolved all his doubt and fear. Such was the awesome power of this profound insight that the Buddha set about trying to communicate it to all those he could interest – and he did so through his presence, through his behaviour, and through the formulation and clear exposition of what became known as "the path", or "way".

Much of what the Buddha said and did is contained in the scriptures that have been handed down from one generation of followers to the next. Initially these were transmitted orally, the monks having regularly recited and memorized the words of the Buddha. Later, monks began to write them down on palm leaves, subsequently they were preserved in print and now they are available electronically.

Towards "wholeness"

The Buddha's teachings and their historical basis have much less importance to Buddhists than do the scriptures based on revelation for those who are believers of the monotheistic Abrahamic religions. The reasons for this need to be understood clearly in order to avoid a trap that exists: thinking that the teachings represent truth rather than serving merely as a map or guide that will enable people to arrive at wholeness. The teachings are therefore, in part, a manual of "how to", as well as a description of the sights and landmarks on the journey towards freedom and emancipation – in short, they offer a method.

> If you wish to know the taste of seawater and you live on an island, set out towards the coast and keep going. When you reach the seashore all you then need to do is to bend down, put the finger into the water, and then into the mouth and you will know the taste of all the seven seas. So it is with freedom, it has but one single taste.
>
> RINZAI ZEN MASTER HAKUIN (1685–1768)

Wonderful though this description is, people need to receive the inspiration that will make them take that first step on their journey – and having started it is all too easy to give up or get lost on the way. When a person uses a journey-planning device before setting out on a long trek, it is necessary to know where they are starting from; orientation is also an important feature in the Buddha's teachings.

From experience to enlightenment

The Buddha starts from the inner world of experience and never really deviates from that, but because humans are endowed with bodies located in space and time the *sutras* (*sutta*s, P.) also reflect the cultural landscape of the era during which the Buddha lived. Thus it is important to separate out purely local ways of framing things from the universal elements of human experience. For example, in the Buddha's day the Vedic traditions were generally accepted, and these included: a belief in a creator deity, a cosmology of gods and heavens, the practice of sacrifice and ritual administered by a priestly caste acting as intermediaries between people and the gods, and the idea of rebirth. This set of beliefs, inherited by the Buddha, was reflected in some of the earliest sacred utterances ever recorded:

> He who by his might looked even over the waters
> Which held power and generated the sacrificial fire
> He who alone is God to whom shall we offer our sacrifice?

THE RIG VEDA

Reincarnation is erroneously thought to be the central idea of Buddhism, but the Buddha's path is actually concerned with life in *this* body in *this* life. "Rebirth" is not about reincarnation as an ant or a god, but the fear of life as an endless round of suffering without the possibility of change.

The idea of the teachings as pure, life-giving water is contained in the original insight of the Buddha on his enlightenment. Insight is not actually the best word, and "life-changing experience" is not quite right either, but the alteration that took place was one during which Siddhartha the sincere prince ceased being a seeker and became someone who had arrived – a *buddha* (from *bodhi* to awake, thus the Buddha is "the awakened one") who had found the answer to his quest. In Pali and Sanskrit he is called Tathāgata, or "Thus Come".

The enlightenment, or *nirvana* (*nibbana*, P.), of Siddhartha Gautama is an event beyond words, just as a musical chord is best heard rather than being discussed. *Nirvana* is something that can be attained by all human beings, and the historical Buddha – as Siddhartha became known – merely drew a map that would enable others to follow him. For all who adhere to the teachings it is possible to have at least a taste of freedom, and a glimpse of another way of being and living – one unencumbered by the cares and anxieties with which we load ourselves. Like tasting the salty sea, we too can discern something of the Buddha's insight, but to become completely immersed in it is another matter that requires a much greater level of commitment, though that too is possible.

Rediscoverer of an ancient path

The Buddha spent the rest of his life teaching others to find release from their sufferings, as he had. During that phase he brought many to an understanding of the nature of suffering and the way out of suffering. Among his early disciples were kings, princes, nobles, *brahmin*s, many holy men, merchants, householders, and even criminals.

He is said to have been one in a long line of *buddhas*, or enlightened awakened beings, and there will be others to follow him – for example, Maitreya – in the future. Rather than being uniquely in possession of a truth, the Buddha was said to have "rediscovered an ancient path to an ancient city". He did not claim to have sole access to an omnipotent and omniscient being; instead, like a trailblazer, he had reopened a way that had simply become overgrown. "City" represents a place of civilization, safety, refuge and nourishment – it is a symbol of human cultivation and harmony that contrasts with a hazard-laden journey through the wilderness, during which one is prey to wild beasts, brigands and many other risks.

These two themes, of wilderness and civilization in its fullness, recur in Buddhism, as do many other opposites of this kind. The idea of taming and cultivating a wild and unruly heart that is full of emotions and passions, driven by both the highest ideals and at the same time subject to the most base and grasping motivation, remains a concept that is paramount.

The teachings recognize that the state of fear, alienation

and meaninglessness that afflicts human beings can be resolved. The journey is one that takes individuals from isolation and loneliness and all that is part of the existential malaise of humankind back to our origins in this human body to find the happiness that is our birthright.

The truth lies within

> . . . in this very body, six feet in length, with its sense-impressions, thoughts and ideas, lies the world, the origin of the world, the ending of the world, and likewise the way that leads to the cessation of the world.

ANGUTTARA NIKAYA

One of the earliest sayings of the Buddha, this quote is part of a much longer one where a sage asks the Buddha where liberation is to be found? Rather than naming an extraterrestrial location, such as a heaven, the Buddha states clearly that it is within us that can be found both the origin of and solution to suffering – it is not in some imagined space, nor is it to be put off until after death.

There is no indication that there is a body without a mind, nor a mind without a body, but that the two are inseparably linked. The duality of mind and body, as if they could be separate entities, does not arise. There is no mind without a body and no body without a mind.

An unchanged core of teachings

During the two and a half millennia since the Buddha's passing, the core teachings have remained unchanged despite the emergence of newer schools and traditions alongside the oldest and most conservative ones. These teachings start with the simple observation that life is mostly suffering: old age is suffering, sickness is suffering, and dying is suffering; wanting to have something I can not have is suffering, wanting to escape from what I do not like is suffering, and having to part with what I like is suffering. All this is caused by a single root – desire.

> I have known pleasure and the limitations of pleasure.
>
> THE BUDDHA (TRADITIONAL)

We can be fortunate and pass much of our life doing more or less what we want, but sooner or later we come up against a problem: How do we react to situations that do not go our way? Very often with little skill, and less patience, thus sadly we learn little from such reverses but soldier on, bloodied and unbowed, to the next encounter where we fare no better. Alternatively, we may succeed and go from success to success, but before we know it we become quite carried away by a sense of self-importance.

Every difficulty is an opportunity to practise and learn. The Buddha's teachings enable us not only to take disappointment and success in our stride, but also to act with skill, so that everything becomes an opportunity, sometimes to learn but always to move forward. This process of coming to terms with life's events has, over time, a profoundly beneficial effect on almost every level of our existence, as well as on those whom we have contact with.

"The frog in the pond knows little of the great ocean", so goes a Zen saying, and if we are honest, generally we are not very conscious or aware. Much of our time is spent only on our own small concerns, and we are victims of our wishes and whims, fears and desires, which diminish us. Sometimes, despite ourselves, we suddenly become conscious of a much bigger world. Profoundly moving experiences do this to us, as do quiet moments when the anxieties and concerns of life fall away and something else opens out. Although such moments often fade quickly, we can learn to enter this

timeless space through cultivation, attention and "letting go". It is the habit patterns that we are almost completely unaware of that keep us chained.

The path to awareness

When we become truly aware of our negative ways of behaving, it is a natural inclination to want to change them. Once our energy is no longer discharged blindly, a transformation begins to take place gradually. When difficult situations arise we no longer become impatient and react with hostility. When a wonderful thing happens we don't get "puffed up". More importantly still, we cease to be a burden on those around us and become a source of comfort and strength to them.

The heart longs for fulfilment and this can not be found in the accumulation of things material. On the contrary, we must divest ourselves of attachment. The way of the Buddha is the shedding of such attachments – to "me" and "mine", to me the "person" and then the "being", and finally the most difficult thing of all to give up, but which we all must, the attachment to life itself. This does not mean living in poverty, but letting go of the grasping attachments that skew reality. If we need a single word, it is pride that sets us up and apart from all things including our own nature.

To be humble and to be good releases untold energy, and to have the strength to be humble and good is not easy for people. The way of the Buddha is a method for doing this.

> To do only good, to avoid doing harm, to empty the heart is the way of all the Awakened.
>
> THE DHAMMAPADA – VERSE 183 OF CHAPTER 14,
> "THE BUDDHA (THE AWAKENED)"

By letting go of what we hold dear, we partake in reality just as it is. If we judge and compare, pick and choose, then we try only to do or experience or feel what appeals to us and we avoid all the difficult bits. The result is a half-lived life.

How are we to redress this imbalance in our nature? We can look for inspiration to the life experience of someone who has gone before us and found a solution to personal unhappiness, in this case the Buddha.

When something wonderful happens to us, we want to share it with others. So it was with the Buddha. He spent the rest of his life after his enlightenment trying to inform others about the path that he had followed. His teachings were disseminated throughout Asia, from Tibet and Thailand to China, Korea and Japan, where the cultures of East Asia added their own influence to the formulation of the Dharma (Dhamma being the Pali equivalent), as the Buddha's teachings are known.

The Life of the Buddha

Siddhartha Gautama was born into the Shakya clan at Kapilvastu, in the foothills of the Himalayas, sometime between 563 and 483 BCE. His father was Suddhodhana Gautama, ruler of a small kingdom on the banks of the Rohini river. His mother, Queen Maya, was the daughter of an uncle on his father's side, who was also a Shakya king.

A magical birth

Although there is little dispute that Siddhartha actually existed, accounts of his life are a blend of historical fact with legend. There has been a great deal of symbolic interpretation and eight principal events have been identified, the first being his birth as a prince. One story relates that Queen Maya – who had been childless for twenty years – had a dream in which she saw a white elephant entering her womb through the right side of her body, signifying that this was no ordinary conception. As the time approached for her to give birth she set out to return to her mother's home, as was the custom. During her journey she rested in the Lumbini Garden. There it is said she reached out with her right arm to pick a spray of Ashoka blossom and, while holding on to it, the prince was suddenly born from her side. The new-born took ten steps in each of the cardinal directions and, with one hand pointing to the earth and the other to the heavens, he proclaimed: "In heaven and on earth, I alone am the world honoured one."

The boy was named Siddhartha, which means "Every wish fulfilled". Asita, a hermit who lived in the hills, realized that a child had been born to the king and queen. He predicted that the prince would be either a great world ruler or a mighty sage: a *buddha* who would save the world. From that moment an edict prohibited Siddhartha from leaving the palace, to prevent his exposure to the harsh realities of life and to ensure the young man grew into a great ruler.

The seeds of spiritual suffering

Queen Maya died a few days after giving birth and her sister Mahaprajapati raised the prince to manhood. Several childhood incidents stand out. At a ploughing ceremony directed by his father the prince drifted off into a state of oneness; it is said that the sun stood still for hours so that the shadow of the rose apple tree under which he sat would remain on him – a memory of this incident, so it goes, led to his enlightenment years later. Another event was seeing a bird carry off a worm, which made him ask: "Alas, must all things die?" His first awareness of impermanence and death.

Siddhartha married but it did not still his questioning nature. After a number of attempts, he managed to leave the palace grounds four times. For the first time he saw, on different occasions, an old man, a sick man, a corpse (the three messengers of old age, sickness and death), and a wandering holy man whose sublime appearance implied he had transcended the fear of death. These "four sights" are said to have been what finally prompted the prince to question his life and embark on a spiritual quest.

Searching for enlightenment

It was the birth of Siddhartha's son, Rahula, that provided the final catalyst for his departure from the palace.

> Being myself subject to decay, disease, death,
> sorrow and the impurities, and seeing the
> disadvantage of being subject to such things,
> what if I were to search after the untainted,
> unsurpassed, perfect security, which is *nirvana*.
>
> MAJJHIMA NIKAYA

Siddhartha had "gone forth" into homelessness. He found two great teachers under whom to study. He then moved on, travelling to the forests of Uruvilva together with five disciples. He undertook severe austerities, almost to the point of death, before he concluded that it was futile.

> All the feelings, sharp, painful, grievous and bitter
> that recluses and *brahmin*s in past times have felt
> – surely these pains of mine go far beyond them
> all. . . . Yet by all this bitter, woeful way, do I not
> achieve the excellence of knowledge and insight
> surpassing mortal things? Maybe there is some
> other way to wisdom.
>
> MAJJHIMA NIKAYA

A local maiden, Sujata, offered Siddhartha a bowl of rice and milk. He accepted and determined to find a saner way. His five companions left him, complaining that he had taken to luxuries. He was completely alone. He remembered the childhood episode under the rose apple tree and it occurred to him that such calm stillness might be the means.

With no status, no family, no friends, Siddhartha entered a meditative state to realize his quest. After many days, on the final night, he met and was unmoved by not only the blissful state of the *dhyana*s (*jhana*s, P.) but also the onslaught of the demon-king Mara, who tempted him with duty (urging him to return to the palace and take up his responsibilities) and with sensual pleasure (in the form of his beautiful daughters), as well as with terror (in the form of demons). In reviewing all his previous births and deaths in an endless round, the prince discovered the causes of birth and death, desire and intentional action. The nature of causation was made plain to him and it is said that he looked up, saw the morning star and attained full enlightenment. He had become the Buddha, or "Awakened One".

> Just as a rock of one solid mass remains unshaken by the wind, even so neither visible forms, nor sounds, nor colours, nor tastes, nor bodily impressions, neither the desired nor the undesired, can cause such a one to waver. Steadfast is his mind, gained is deliverance.
>
> ANGUTTARA NIKAYA

He spent the rest of his life teaching, and establishing the monastic community of monks and nuns. His family, who had been estranged from him, became his supporters. He continued to preach until his last moment, when, at the age of eighty, his last words to his disciples were:

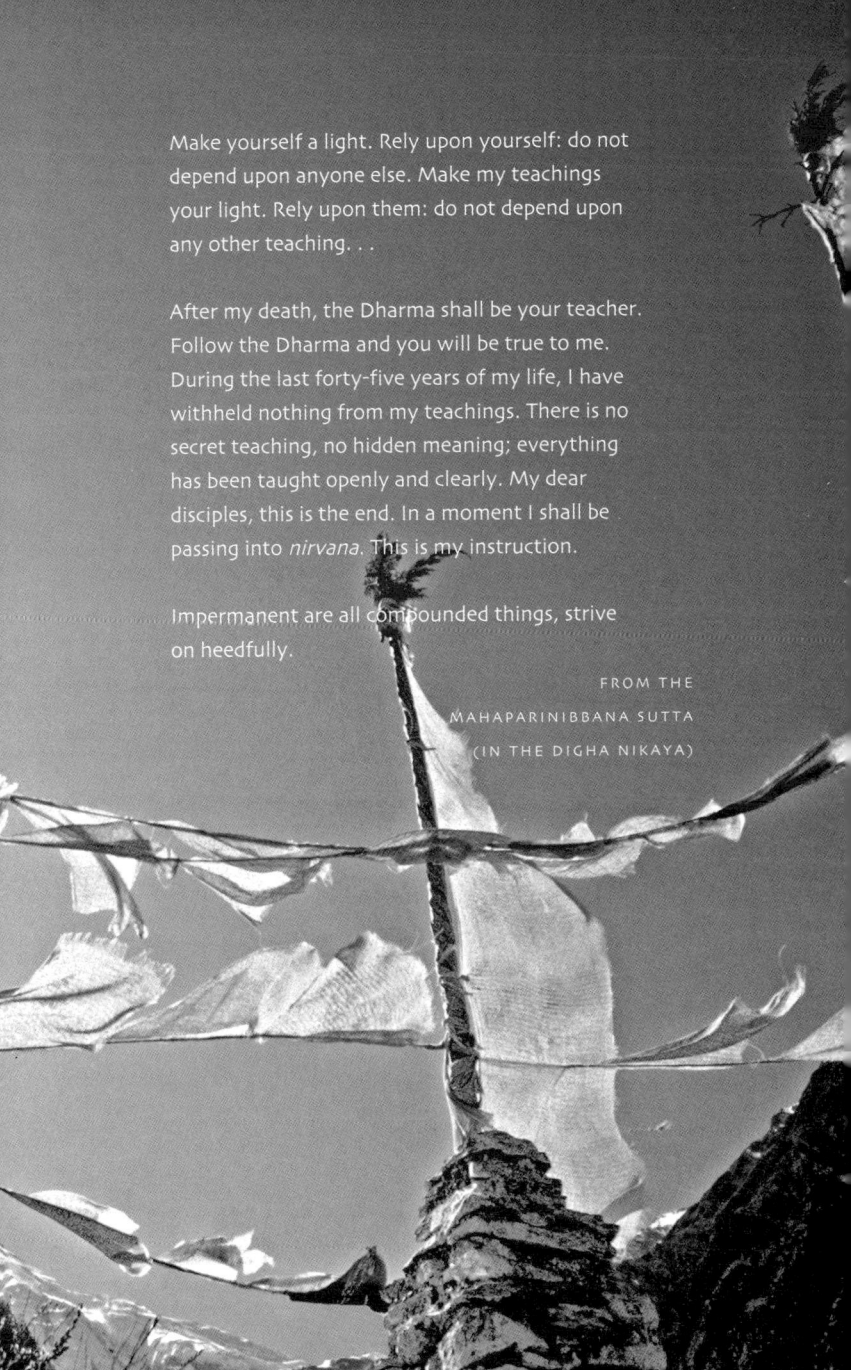

Make yourself a light. Rely upon yourself: do not depend upon anyone else. Make my teachings your light. Rely upon them: do not depend upon any other teaching. . .

After my death, the Dharma shall be your teacher. Follow the Dharma and you will be true to me. During the last forty-five years of my life, I have withheld nothing from my teachings. There is no secret teaching, no hidden meaning; everything has been taught openly and clearly. My dear disciples, this is the end. In a moment I shall be passing into *nirvana*. This is my instruction.

Impermanent are all compounded things, strive on heedfully.

FROM THE
MAHAPARINIBBANA SUTTA
(IN THE DIGHA NIKAYA)

The scriptural sources

There are many collections of Buddhist texts, and a summary of the principal ones is set out below. Buddhism lacks a single authoritative language, but some scholars group the texts according to the main languages in which they have been compiled: Pali, Sanskrit, Chinese, Korean, Japanese or other languages no longer in use, such as Khotanese. Others organize the texts by country and geographical region: Tibet, China, Korea, Japan, Burma, Southeast Asia, East Asia or quite simply as the two very broad divisions of the schools of Southern Buddhism and Northern Buddhism, equating to the Theravada tradition and the Mahayana tradition respectively.

The oral instructions of the Buddha that form the doctrinal foundation of Theravada Buddhism, its most traditional form (*thera* means "elder", *vada* means "way"), are recorded in a collection of texts, with the only complete surviving version being that written in Pali. The collection has a threefold division and is known as the "Three Baskets" (Tipitaka in Pali, Tripitaka in Sanskrit). The Tipitaka consists of teachings about monastic discipline (Vinaya Pitaka), discourses attributed to the Buddha and his early followers (Sutta Pitaka), and more abstract texts that deal with higher teachings and philosophies (Abhidhamma Pitaka). This Pali canon is that observed by those countries that follow the Theravada tradition, such as Sri Lanka, Burma, Thailand and other countries of Southeast Asia.

After the Buddha's death his followers came together to recite his words and set them down. Ananda, the personal attendant of the Buddha who had been present through much of his teaching life, made a considerable contribution, but was only one among many who contributed. In the years that followed there developed many slightly different versions of the teachings in various languages. Each was identified with a particular sect or early school, and there were eighteen of those in all.

After several centuries new *sutra* texts began to appear in monasteries, mainly in the north. These were given the name of "greater" (*maha*) teaching, later to be called the Mahayana teachings (*yana* means "vehicle" or "way" in Sanskrit). In these texts there began to emerge a new understanding of the Buddha's message, perhaps best exemplified in the idea of universal compassion and the *bodhisattva* (*bodhisatta*, P.) ideal – that of not seeking final release until all beings down to the last blade of grass had reached enlightenment. These scriptures also included the earliest teachings of the Buddha, as well as new ways of seeing the Dharma, and the adherents began to call themselves the Mahayana school. At no time did the followers exclude the earliest teachings, but they designated them, somewhat disparagingly, to be *hina* (meaning "small" or "lesser") teachings. The Mahayana was a more devotional form of Buddhism and it elevated texts to a new level of importance. Its earliest thought is arguably best revealed in the Lotus Sutra, Pure Land *sutra*s and the corpus known as the Prajnaparamita (the Perfection of Wisdom *sutra*s).

The Tipitaka
Vinaya Pitaka

This translates as "The Basket of Monastic Discipline" and is commonly referred to as the Vinaya. It is concerned with the rules for the Sangha, or monastic community, both ordained and lay. It divides into three parts: the Suttavibhanga, which contains a set of rules for monks and nuns known as the

Patimokkha (Pratimoksha, S.); the Khandhaka, which includes sections on the life of the Buddha and detailing responsibilities and rules for rituals; and the Parivara, which gives summaries that help to instruct new members.

Sutta Pitaka

The "Basket of Discourses" is the largest part of the Tipitaka, with more than thirty volumes of *suttas* (*sutra*s) grouped into five collections (*nikaya*s): the Digha Nikaya ("Group of Long Discourses"), the Majjhima Nikaya ("Group of Medium-Length Discourses"), the Samyutta Nikaya ("Group of Connected Discourses"), the Anguttara Nikaya ("Group of Discourses Arranged Numerically in Ascending Order") and the Khuddaka Nikaya ("Group of Small Texts"). The latter is a miscellaneous collection that comprises fifteen books, which includes the influential Dhammapada ("Verses of the Dharma") and the Jataka ("Birth Stories").

Abhidamma Pitaka

The "Basket of Scholastic Doctrine" comprises seven books, which are systematic analyses of phenomena and higher teachings. These are profound and valuable but difficult for most people to comprehend. The seven are as follows: the Dhammasangani ("Enumeration of Phenomena"), the Vibhanga ("Book of Treatises"), the Dhatukatha ("Discussion Concerning the Elements"), the Puggalapannati ("Description of Individuals"), the Kathavatthu ("Points of Controversy"), the Yamaka ("Books of Pairs") and the Patthana ("Book of Relations").

The Mahayana teachings

Developed over time, these teachings do not deny and are

never in conflict with the early sayings and teachings of the Buddha contained in the Pali Canon – among the early texts of Buddhism the Mahayana equivalent of the *nikaya*s are the *agama*s. Of the approximately 600 Mahayana *sutra*s, these exist either in the original Sanskrit and Prakrit or were long ago translated into Chinese, Tibetan, Korean or Japanese (see below). However, a distinguishing feature of the *sutra*s is the fact that many of them were written later and other schools claim that these are not actual historical teachings but additions, albeit ones which adhere to the spirit of the Buddha.

The Prajnaparamita

This is a class of literature, the Perfection of Wisdom *sutra*s, that deals with conceptions of the cosmos and humankind's relation to it, with a particular emphasis on wisdom as a virtue. Outlining the earliest Mahayana thought, among the Prajnaparamita's most popular *sutra*s are the Heart Sutra and the Diamond Sutra (see below).

Sukhavativyuha Sutra

Three Pure Land texts share this title, which translates from the Sanskrit as "Describing the World of Bliss Sutra". The first two are the Shorter Sukhavativyuha Sutra and the Longer Sukhavativyuha Sutra. The third has several titles, the simplest of which is the "Contemplation Sutra".

Vajrachedika Prajnaparamita Sutra

The "Diamond Sutra" is the oldest surviving printed work (868CE) and was recovered from Dunhuang. A short work, it is often memorized and chanted by monks. It consists of a dialogue about the nature of perception.

Vimalakirti Nirdesa Sutra

This *sutra* is about the doctrine of emptiness and its mastery by a lay believer. The original has long been lost and two of the best surviving translations are considered to be those of the fourth-century Turfan scholar Kumarajiva and the mid-seventh century Chinese monk Xuanzang.

Saddharma Pundarika

The "White Lotus of the True Law" is better known as the Lotus Sutra. This long scripture had a profound impact in Central and East Asia – at one time seventeen different translations existed in China. The *sutra* contains many popular and frequently quoted parables, such as "The Burning House" (see page 38), and was the doctrinal basis for the Tiantai (Tendai in Japan) sect in the sixth century.

Avatamsaka Sutra

The Flower Garland, or Flower Ornament, Sutra was the core text of China's highly intellectual Huayan schools, which claimed it as the highest form of truth in existence. Mahayana tradition considers it the first sermon of the Buddha after his enlightenment.

The Tibetan Canon

In addition to early Buddhist and Mahayana texts, the scriptures of Tibet include a body of writings called *tantra*s (the texts belonging to the Vajrayana, or Diamond Vehicle, form of Tantric Buddhism distinctive to Tibet, which is said to have arisen from the third turning of the wheel of the Dharma at Shravasti).

The canon is organized into two categories, the Kangyur ("Translated Words") and the Tengyur ("Translated

Treatises"). The Kangyur includes the Prajnaparamita, the Avatamsaka Sutra and other Mahayana *sutra*s, as well as Nikaya texts and sections of the Vinaya – there are about 100 volumes in all. The Tengyur is a supplement containing Abhidamma works, treatises and commentaries, making up more than 3,600 texts in 224 volumes.

The spread of the teachings

In India the Buddha's five companions became his first followers after his enlightenment and he presented to them the basic teachings of The Middle Way, The Four Noble Truths and The Noble Eightfold Path. His followers also took his teachings far and wide. One influential devotee was the Mauryan ruler Ashoka (reigned 273–232BCE) who sent out missions as far afield as Macedonia and Syria. King Ashoka was also responsible for sending a monk to Sri Lanka, where Buddhism became firmly established.

Of the Buddha's first disciples, two were merchants from Burma and it was along the overland and transoceanic trade routes that Theravada Buddhism, or the "Doctrine of the Elders", was to spread to all of Southeast Asia, a path known as the "southern transmission". To the north of India, via Gandhara (the upper Indus region) and Tibet, there lay the vast territories of Central Asia, connected eastwards to Turfan and westwards to Bactria by the Silk Road. It was along this "northern transmission" route that the teachings of the Buddha reached China, and eventually to Mongolia, Vietnam, Korea and Japan.

China

Buddhism reached China in the first century CE and a process of translation began that was to last eight centuries. In

399CE a group of Chinese Buddhist monks, including Faxian, went on a pilgrimage to India to obtain texts. Several centuries later, in order to complete the translation process, another epic journey was undertaken by Xuanzang. As a result of these hundreds of years of effort, Chinese amassed a vast body of texts, which were woodblock-printed and disseminated throughout East Asia.

Chinese Buddhism developed new Mahayana schools, such as Chan, Tiantai and Pure Land. Chan was founded in China by the Indian scholar Bodhidharma in the early sixth century. Chan was a reforming movement and looked not to scripture but to a life of simplicity, meditative practice and the cultivation of the mind to attain enlightenment. It attained its highest development in Japan, as Zen. The Tiantai school was founded in the late sixth century and it held the Lotus Sutra to be the most complete expression of Buddhist truth. The Pure Land was inspired by the Nirvana Sutra and owed much to the development of salvific ideas by Tanluan and Daochuo, from the fifth to seventh centuries.

After the Mongols invaded China in the late thirteenth century, the Tibetan form of Buddhism became dominant in China and other sects declined. Chan survived by merging with the Pure Land.

Japan

Buddhism reached Japan in the sixth century when King Song of Korea sent an envoy (in 538CE) to present a Buddhist scroll of *sutra*s to the imperial court of Emperor Kinmei of Japan. Just a decade earlier the kingdom of Silla had recognized Buddhism as the state religion of Korea, having noticed how effectively the faith had strengthened the nation in China. In a similar way, Buddhism transformed

Japan: temples became important social centres and an important culture, not merely a religion, developed.

The most famous school of Japanese Buddhism is Zen, which is a development of Chan from China. Japan's renowned tea ceremony, temple gardens, calligraphy, poetry, and so on, were all developed from Zen practice. The two largest schools of Zen are Rinzai and Soto, which both emphasize a seated form of meditation known as *zazen*.

The Japanese monk Eisai (1141–1215) returned from China and introduced Rinzai, as well as tea, to Japan. It was a form of Buddhism that appealed to the élite warrior class or samurai. This form of Zen stresses the *koan* system of difficult questions as an element of training. These are questions that cannot be answered by the intellect alone but by insight – an approach that owes much to the energy of the Rinzai master Hakuin (1685–1768). To answer a *koan* can take years of training – and once answered the master, or *roshi*, may put the question to the student once again.

The much larger Soto school typically makes less use of *koan*s and of meetings with masters. Its approach to practice is more patient and structured by rules. Dogen (1200–1253), who founded the Soto school, advocated diligent and deep solitary meditation, known as *shikan-taza* ("just sitting") – he wrote:

> You should stop pursuing words and letters,
> and learn to withdraw and reflect on yourself.
> When you do so, your body and mind will fall
> away naturally and your original *buddha*-nature
> will appear.
>
> FROM THE SHOBOGENZO ("THE EYE OF THE TRUE LAW") BY DOGEN

Under the leadership of an ex-Tendai (as Tiantai was known in Japan) monk called Honen (1133–1212), Pure Land Buddhism became an independent sect in Japan. It was known as Jodo Shu and dominated alongside Zen.

Tibet

Despite its proximity to northern India, across the Himalayas, Tibet was not to be exposed to Buddhism until a millennia after the time of the Buddha. It arrived in two waves. The first, in the seventh and eighth centuries, is called the Nyingma, or the "ancient school". The second, between the tenth and thirteenth centuries, is the Sarma or "new translation" period.

Three so-called "Dharma Kings" were instrumental in establishing Buddhism in Tibet. Familiarity began with the Nepalese wives of King Songtsen Gampo (r.620–649), but the process received a more significant boost in the eighth century when King Trisong Detsen (r.754–797) invited Shantarakshita, an Indian teacher, to establish a monastery, which he did at Samye with the aid of Padmasmbhava.

When Trisong's Yarlung empire began to disintegrate in the ninth century Buddhism remained of limited interest in a land already with a religion in the form of Bon. However, in 1042 the arrival of an Indian teacher called Atisha, who had learned Tibetan, heralded a second propagation. Atisha emphasized the devotion that disciples needed to have for masters, hence the importance of applying the ideals of a *bodhisattva* in the practitioner's life.

Monastic discipline, more arcane practices (partly under the influence of Bon) and the pre-eminent role enjoyed by various adepts and teachers – such as the *siddha*s, *tulku*s and *lama*s, notably the Dalai Lama – have done much to shape Tibetan Buddhism. The esoteric strand of the religion is called Vajrayana ("Diamond Thunderbolt Vehicle", sometimes called The Third Turning of the Wheel of the Dharma – after Theravada/Hinayana and Mahayana), also known as Tantra, and it is highly characteristic of Tibet. Vajrayana is based on writings called *tantra*s, which set out a path by means of which it is possible to achieve *buddha*hood in a short time, not by philosophical doctrines but complex practices of visualization which utilize highly developed hierarchies of deities.

Europe and North America

The Western world encountered Buddhism as a result of the era of European colonial expansion in Asia, which saw the emergence of a body of learned travellers, historians, scholars and linguists fascinated by the history and religions of ancient India and the cultures of the Far East. From the nineteenth century onwards, Britain was the leading centre for much of the research into Eastern religious writings and the foundation of the Royal Asiatic Society (1824), the Pali Text Society (1881), the School of Oriental Studies (1916) and The Buddhist Society (1924), all reflected public interest. The first Buddhist temples in the West were built to provide for compatriots overseas, but interest on the part of Westerners began after the World's Parliament of Religions in Chicago in 1893. The first Buddhist denomination to establish itself outside Asia was a Japanese Pure Land denomination, which built temples in Hawaii and California.

In more than a century since then Buddhism has attracted hundreds of thousands of Westerners as followers, and interest in it continues to grow. There are hundreds of different schools of Buddhism and Buddhist centres now

established in the West, but irrespective of the school, tradition or style everything comes back to the core teachings of the Buddha, as set out here in the chapters that follow.

> Your suffering is my suffering and your happiness is my happiness.
>
> THE BUDDHA (TRADITIONAL)

About this book

Just as a good doctor takes down a proper personal history and then makes a thorough examination before determining the cure, the Buddha also diagnoses the patient's ailment and offers a treatment plan. His teachings come in two parts: the first offers the description of the condition, both impersonal and personal, that gives rise to our suffering, and the second proposes the remedy.

In Chapter One these conditions are described by looking at the "twelve-linked chain of causation", or what is sometimes called the "doctrine of dependent origination". The universal laws that describe all existence, the "three signs of being", are the subject of Chapter Two. The "three fires" are described in Chapter Three; although these are found universally within all living beings, humans are the only living creatures to be able to become aware of them and thus to change.

When it comes to "the cure", the universal and impersonal gives way to the teachings. Chapter Four deals with "The Middle Way", which is the most important of all the Buddha's teachings and the one from which all others are derived. Chapter Five explains "The Four Noble Truths" and Chapter Six looks at "The Noble Eightfold Path", the practical guide to living. Chapter Seven is a guide to the practice of the *paramita*s ("perfections"), the skilful way of living that can remove suffering and lead to a happy, energetic engagement with life. In Chapter Eight the essential cultivation of practice and the development of form are examined. Chapter Nine looks at the cultivation of mindfulness, without which transformation is not possible. Chapter Ten is a look at meditation in all its aspects.

The Burning House

> Once there lived a wealthy man whose house caught fire. He was away from home and when he came back he found his children were so absorbed in play that they had not noticed the fire was raging. He screamed: "Get out children! Come out of the house! Hurry!" But they did not heed him. He shouted again: "Children I have some wonderful toys here, come out of the house and get them!" Heeding his cry this time, the children ran out of the burning house to be entertained by the toys he had brought.
>
> THE LOTUS SUTRA

The Mahayana *sutra*s make use of all manner of literary devices – allegory, metaphor, tales within tales, fantastical settings, and so on – to convey a teaching. In this story, the toys that the father had brought to tempt the children out were carriages, very decorative and attractive, which symbolize the vehicles that are the teachings. Although the children were not aware of the danger they were in, just as we are ignorant of the danger we are in from desire and craving, the Buddha has, out of great compassion, put together the teachings so that, like toys, we might be attracted to them, will study them and thereby escape the certain dangers of attachment.

The world is a burning house says the Buddha. We are not aware that the house is on fire and we are in danger of being burned alive because we are wedded to wordly pleasures. But through compassionate teachings we can be saved. These playthings (the teachings) will save us despite ourselves.

The Teachings

The Twelve-Linked Chain of Causation

The Dharma teachings reveal that the "universal law" or Dharma (Dhamma, P.) is vast, impersonal and neutral. The *pratitya–samutpada* or "twelve-linked chain of causation" (*paticcasamuppada*, P.) represents, in its earliest formulation, the interlinked and interlocked series of events that arise from ignorance and lead to sickness, suffering, old age and death. Although this doctrine appears to be easy to understand, Ananda, the Buddha's attendant, was admonished for assuming it to be straightforward. This is how the teaching was recorded in the Sutta Pitaka:

> Thus have I heard: On a certain occasion the Exalted One was staying at Uruvela, on the bank of the Neranjara river at the foot of the bodhi-tree, having just won the highest wisdom.
>
> Now on that occasion the Exalted One was seated for seven days in one posture and experienced the bliss of release. Then the Exalted One, after a lapse of those seven days during the first watch of the night, rousing himself from that first concentration of mind, gave close attention to causal uprising in direct order, thus: This being, that becomes; by the arising of this, that arises – namely: conditioned by ignorance, activities; conditioned by activities, consciousness; conditioned by consciousness, mind and body; conditioned by mind and body,

the six sense spheres; conditioned by the six sense spheres, contact; conditioned by contact, feeling; conditioned by feeling, craving; conditioned by craving, grasping; conditioned by grasping, becoming; conditioned by becoming, birth; conditioned by birth, old age and death, grief, lamentation, suffering, sorrow and despair come into being. Thus arises this mass of ill.

Thereupon the Exalted One, seeing the meaning of it, uttered this verse of uplift:
"When things become plain to the ardent, musing *brahmin*,
All his doubts vanish, since he knows 'thing-with-its-cause'."

THE UDANA (IN THE KHUDDAKA NIKAYA)

The first of the twelve links, or fetters (*nidana*s), in the continuous chain is "ignorance". Although it is listed "first" it is not actually a primal cause because it too has its causes, namely old age and death. The chain is in fact a continuous one that is normally presented as a circle or wheel. The first and second links represent past life, the third to seventh are the rebirth process, the eighth to tenth represent the *karma*-producing process (*karma-bhava*), and the eleventh and twelfth represent the rebirth process.

The wheel of conditioning ceases only when the cycle is interrupted at links eight to ten. If death breaks the chain, the inherent *karma* (*kamma*, P.) will lead to a new life with ignorance from the previous life.

Each link in the chain is usually represented in a particular way. The first link, of ignorance (*avidya/avijja*), is usually

symbolized by a blind person; the second, volition (*samskhara/sankhara*), by a potter at his wheel; the third, consciousness (*vijnana/vinnana*), by a monkey in a tree; the fourth, mind and body (*nama-rupa*), is represented by two people in a boat; the fifth, the six senses (*sadayatana/ayatana*), by an empty house with windows; the sixth, contact (*sparsa/phassa*), is shown by a couple embracing; the seventh, feeling (*vedana*), by an arrow piercing an eye; the eighth, craving or desire (*trsna/tanha*), is indicated by a person drinking; the ninth, grasping, (*upadana*) by a person gathering fruit; the tenth, becoming (*bhava*), is symbolized by a pregnant woman; the eleventh, birth (*jati*), by a woman giving birth; and the twelfth, old age (*jaramarana*), is represented by an elderly person with a corpse.

The chain can be broken or interrupted only through the cultivation of awareness

by working with "the three fires" (also known as poisons, hindrances, or cankers – see chapter four, pages 78–89) of desire, anger and delusion. These "fires" are impersonal in so far as they have a blind elemental quality; they are not me, not mine, No-I (see chapter three, pages 62–77) – but the "I" in each of us can be carried away by them and as a consequence it becomes them.

"I" become enraged, whereupon awareness is obliterated and all sense of perspective is lost. Intoxicated by pleasure, I am blinded; people are heard to say, "I don't know what came over me" – this emotion is attachment and delusion. The "three signs of being" (suffering, impermanence, and No-I) are also impersonal, universal qualities. No state is permanent; this includes such things as a painful illness or a difficult boss, a spell of weather or a happy holiday. Each changes, it has no ultimate essence and as a consequence it is unsatisfactory. The only true release from our attachments and clinging is *nirvana* (*nibbana,* P.), the state that is not subject to conditionality, one in which there is no longer an "I" to cling, to suffer, or to be carried away.

One cosmos

In later teachings of the Mahayana tradition the doctrine of the twelve-linked chain of causation took on a much more universal and cosmic flavour as a result of the development of the *anatman* (*anatta,* P.) doctrine to include everything.

Everything is interconnected, nothing exists independently of anything else, all things are mutually interdependent, and all things arise together. Humans are part of this single, interdependent, universal drama – and, importantly, so too is what goes on in the psycho-physical flux that we call a person.

In the Avatamsaka Sutra, composed in India in about the third century CE, the metaphor of "The Net of Indra" – the great god of the Vedas who lives in a palace on Mount Meru, the *axis mundi* of the universe – is used to describe the interpenetration, mutual interdependence and interconnectedness of all things, not only the material world but the mental and psychic spheres too.

> There is a net of three dimensions, vast and wide stretching in all four directions throughout the universe. At each point that a string meets another point of the net there is a jewel, and this jewel reflects in it all the other jewels of the entire net, and further that reflection too is reflected in all the facets of all the other jewels.
>
> No single part of the net can be independent of the rest; a single movement of the net in one place will affect, in some way, the most distant part of the net or universe. The all is reflected in the one, and the one in the all.

THE AVATAMSAKA SUTRA

(THE FLOWER GARLAND SUTRA)

At around about the same time as the Buddha in India, in ancient Greece there were pre-Socratic philosophers – men such as Thales, Anaximander, Anaximenes and Democritus – who were newly curious about the origins of the universe. They no longer sought to explain the cosmos by a myth or legend but tried instead to find some underlying common principle or substance, such as the elements in different combinations, from which everything arose. They intended to show that the universe, even in diversity, was composed of the same material in different states of combination.

Democritus developed an atomic theory which was not unlike the view of the *dharma*s proposed by the Vaisesika school of early Buddhism (a *dharma* refers to one of the elements rather than the Dharma, or law). But closer still to the later teaching of the Buddha was that of Heraclitus

of Ephesus (ca. 530–475BCE) who taught that change was central to the universe, and the only enduring principle was *logos*. However, Heraclitus offered no application of his teaching whereas for the Buddha the perception of reality just as it is (*dhaamata*), *is* the end of suffering.

These ancient ideas have persisted into the age of modern physics. Big Bang theory proposes that the universe started from a singularity, which mirrors the assertion in the Upanishadic world that the cosmos started as a point known as *bindu*. Thus, the diversity we see is real yet interconnected and consisting of the same "stuff". Whether matter, energy or mind, any kind of assertion that any single part of it is separate, independent and of an enduring independent nature is impossible to maintain.

In Chaos theory the movement of even a butterfly wing in one part of the world sets in motion a series of events that will have unpredictable results in a distant place. The Quantum theory idea of "particle entanglement" is perhaps the closest view of the essential unity of all matter. Current ideas would suggest that the universe will eventually collapse back into a singularity again, in keeping with ancient ideas wherein the flux of coming to be and ceasing to be is the essential insight.

> All compound things are transitory: they grow and they decay.
>
> THE BUDDHA (TRADITIONAL)

Not a cosmologist but a healer

Importantly, the Buddha admonished his disciples from enquiring about such cosmological matters; he considered them irrelevant because his message was not about the coming into being of the material world but the origin of suffering. He said so at a time when there were many cosmogenic theories: one suggesting four phases of the cycle – dissolution, nothingness, creation and duration – each lasting for incalculable aeons in an eternal round of coming to be and ceasing to be. Instead, the Buddha, a radical religious teacher, pointed to the inner universe of the mind, the nature of suffering and its dissolution. According to this theory, suffering arises because of the delusion of an "I" that gives rise to the sense of separation – and fear – and the delusion of a world composed of friend and foe.

This basic flaw in perception gives rise to the three passions of desire, anger and delusion as the individual struggles to satisfy the demands of this mistaken sense of "I". The ability to live in the world of plurality (subject to the opposites of life and death, and the vicissitudes of everyday life), while at the same time becoming part of the unified, non-dual universe (not subject to the opposites of birth and death, and outside time and change) was to be achieved by following the path the Buddha pointed to in his teachings.

> Just as, brethren, a dark blue lotus or a white lotus, born in the water, comes to full growth in the water, rises to the surface and stands unspotted by the water, even so, brethren, the Tathagata, having been born in the world, having come to full growth in the world, passing beyond the world, abides unspotted by the world.
>
> SUTTA NIPATA (IN THE KHUDDAKA NIKAYA)

The Wheel of Life

Each thing is conditional, nothing has independent essence or existence. This doctrine is often represented as "The Wheel of Life", wherein it is not just the links of the chain but all life that is bound in a universal drama that represents the immutable, unerring law of *karma*, cause and effect, and the interconnectedness of all things.

At the middle of such illustrations are three animals – a cockerel, a snake, and a pig or boar – that represent "the three fires" (or poisons, *klesha*s) of desire, anger and delusion. These form the dynamic hub of the wheel because the psychic energy arising from the animals' passions drive the system. At the centre is an empty space representing *nirvana* and *shunyata* (*sunyata*).

Because the cycle of conditioned life is said to consist of constant death and rebirth (*samsara*), the main part of the wheel divides into six realms of existence. There is a realm of the *deva*s, a human realm, an animal realm, a realm of the demigods, a realm peopled by "hungry ghosts", and a hell of unimaginable suffering. This wheel of intentional actions and their consequences is kept in motion through the central delusion of "I" due to actions informed by ignorance, which leads to desire that results in attachment.

When this delusion is absent humans escape the bonds of cause and effect. Deliverance is possible only from the human realm; the heavenly realms continue blissfully until the benefit of the good *karma* of intentional actions runs out and then, according to the laws of *karma*, the next birth is in one of the other worlds.

Each realm is inhabited by a fully enlightened *buddha*, so even if reborn in hell there is a chance for compassion to be shown and deliverance to another realm. People are born and die and are reborn from moment to moment; depending on a person's state of mind, they will be reborn into a hell world, a heavenly world or a human world. However, in the human realm it is possible to become aware and then blind ignorance will no longer condition the next state of mind; it might even be possible to leave the wheel altogether. In the Buddha's words:

> From the ending of ignorance comes the ending of action-volitions. From the ending of action-volitions comes the ending of consciousness. From the ending of consciousness comes the ending of name and shape or form. From the ending of name and shape or form comes the ending of sensation. From the ending of sensation comes the ending of contact. From the ending of contact comes the ending of feelings. From the ending of feelings comes the ending of craving; and from the ending of craving comes the ending of grasping; and from the ending of grasping comes the ending of becoming; and from the ending of becoming comes the ending of birth; and from the ending of birth comes the ending of ageing and death, sorrow and grief, woe, lamentation, and despair. Such is the ending of all this mass of suffering.
>
> SUTTA NIPATA (IN THE KHUDDAKA NIKAYA)

Karma

The law of *karma*, referring to volitional actions in a moral sense, arises from a thorough understanding of the twelve-linked chain. Just as science has demonstrated the law of cause and effect in the physical world, the Buddha understood that all life in the universe was subject to moral causality. If a person performs an action with a secret but malign intention it will have consequences of a far-reaching nature that will affect the person's happiness and the happiness of others in the future.

> People are obsessed by the notions "done by me" and "done by another". They do not understand that these are harmful thoughts. They do not see them as thorns. But to one who sees, who has extracted the thorns, the ideas "done by me" and "done by another" do not occur.
>
> THE UDANA (IN THE KHUDDAKA NIKAYA)

This law of causality affects people because of the nature of human action that feeds into the interconnected system. How are we to act once we understand that everything we do has an effect on everything else? If I go out without an umbrella and it rains I will get wet. This is the impersonal nature of things and the law of causality in gross material terms. If I blame someone because I forgot my umbrella and spend all day thinking about it, I may suffer far more than from the little bit of rain that fell on me; furthermore, I might then have a row with someone as a consequence.

The simple fact of getting wet is a direct result of the rain falling on me: there is rain, I am under it, I get wet. The law of *karma* is not concerned with that material aspect of causality, but with the inner world: it rains, I do not want to get wet, I do get wet, I get angry because I am wet, I start to blame others, I am in a foul mood, I suffer, so does everyone around me because I am in such a mood. Perusal of the chain will show that it is because of ignorance (*avidya*) that this negative sequence of events comes about, which gives rise to anger and the consequence of that. In this particular case the need to blame will have karmic consequences at some time in the future.

Someone in a lesser state of ignorance will accept that it is raining and even when he or she reacts emotionally to it, if there is awareness there the consequences will be far less dire because the response can be appropriate to the situation. In summary, if I am aware that I am angry, I am less likely to act out; if there is no "I" there to react, just awareness of the rain, there will be no anger at all.

> All that we are is the result of what we have thought: it is founded on our thoughts. If a man speaks or acts with an evil thought, suffering follows him, as the wheel follows the hoof of the beast that draws the wagon.
>
> All that we are is the result of what we have thought: it is founded on our thoughts and made up of our thoughts. If a man speaks or acts with a good thought, happiness follows him like a shadow that never leaves him.
>
> THE DHAMMAPADA – VERSES 1 AND 2
> OF CHAPTER 1, THE "TWIN VERSES"

Willed action is of three kinds

Willed action can be skilful, unskilful or neutral. Unskilful actions arising out of desire, anger and delusion, expressed by body, speech and mind, have negative results and consequences. In contrast, actions arising out of goodwill, liberality and clarity of vision will give rise to good results.

> Intention, monks, is what I call *karma* (action). For through intention one performs the actions of body, speech or mind.
> There is intentional action (*karma*) that ripens in hell.
> There is intentional action (*karma*) that ripens in the animal world.
> There is intentional action (*karma*) that ripens in the human realm.
> There is intentional action (*karma*) that ripens in the heavenly realm.
>
> ANGUTTARA NIKAYA

> All intentional willed action ripens in this life, the next life, or subsequent lives.
>
> ANGUTTARA NIKAYA

> Killing . . . stealing . . . unlawful sexual intercourse . . . lying . . . slandering . . . rude speech . . . foolish babble, if practised, carried on, and frequently cultivated, lead to rebirth in hell, or among the animals, or among the ghosts.
>
> ANGUTTARA NIKAYA

Intentional action *(karma)* always has its results, whether good or bad. Ultimate emancipation comes when actions are no longer intentional but are in keeping with the situation and spontaneous.

> The evil-doer mourns both in this world and the next; he suffers when he sees the results of his misdeeds.
>
> The righteous man rejoices both in this world and the next; he delights and he rejoices when he sees his own good deeds.
>
> The evil-doer suffers both in this world and the next; he suffers when he thinks about the evil he has done, and suffers more when thinking of the evil path ahead.
>
> The righteous man is happy both in this world and the next. He is happy when he thinks about the good that he has done and happier seeing his good path ahead.
>
> THE DHAMMAPADA – VERSES 15–18
> OF CHAPTER 1, THE TWIN VERSES

Unless we as individuals understand that intentional action arises from our need to achieve results, we will continue to suffer for ever – as illustrated in this short extract:

> Now, what do you think? What is the greater, the flood of tears shed by you on this long journey – forever running through the round of birth and death, weeping and wailing because of union with the undesired, because of separation from the desired – or the water of the four mighty oceans?
>
> *Insofar Lord as we understand the teachings, taught by the exalted one, the flood of tears shed by us Lord is greater than all the waters in the four mighty oceans.*
>
> Well said! Well said! And what is the cause?
>
> *No beginning can be seen of those beings hindered by ignorance, bound by craving, forever running through the round of birth and death.*
>
> SUTTA NIPATA (IN THE KHUDDAKA NIKAYA)

However, once this causal connection is understood and awareness takes the place of ignorance, then a great change takes place: action is now free of intention.

> The king of death cannot touch him
> who looks upon the world as a mirage.
>
> THE DHAMMAPADA – VERSE 170
> OF CHAPTER 13, "THE WORLD"

> Look at this glittering world, like a
> royal carriage; the foolish are taken up
> by it, but the wise do not cling to it.
>
> THE DHAMMAPADA – VERSE 171
> OF CHAPTER 13, "THE WORLD"

> The man who overcomes his misdeeds
> with good actions brightens up the world
> like the moon appearing from behind clouds.
>
> THE DHAMMAPADA – VERSE 173
> OF CHAPTER 13, "THE WORLD"

> Even the gods envy him who is
> enlightened and is given to meditation,
> who is free from craving.
>
> THE DHAMMAPADA – VERSE 181
> OF CHAPTER 14, "THE BUDDHA"

> Mere suffering exists, no sufferer is found;
> the deeds are, but no doer of the deeds is there;
> *nirvana* is, but not the man that enters it;
> the path is, but no traveller on it is seen.
>
> FROM THE *VISUDDHIMAGGA* ("PATH TO PURITY'),
> BY BUDDHAGHOSA

The Three Signs of Being

The "three signs of being" are impermanence (*annica/anitya*), suffering (*dukkha/duhka*), and No Soul, Not-Self or No-I (*anatman/anatta*). Known as *trilaksana* (*tilakkhana*, P.), these three "Dharma seals" – also called the "three marks of existence", or "of all experienced phenomena" – are sometimes added to with a fourth, *nirvana*.

The signs reflect the Buddhist world-view that nothing in the universe – no matter how small or how large, no matter the constituents, or how stable something might appear to be – remains the same for even the smallest measurable moment. Everything is in constant change, motion, or flux. Impermanence and No-I apply to all things in the universe and suffering to all that is sensate, conscious or sentient.

The central delusion is that for human beings *things* appear to have an ultimate enduring reality, are of value or supreme importance. This delusion is particularly relevant when it comes to ideas about "me": my sense of identity, my self-esteem (high or low), my individuality, my values, and so on. If asked, many people will deny having any belief in a soul or some enduring identity, and yet they behave exactly as though they do. Most religions support a belief in an ultimate surviving entity or spirit that will endure after death, often called a soul in English (*atman* in Sanskrit: *an* means "no", hence *anatman* means "no soul").

Early Vedic religion in India stated that the object of religious endeavour was the ultimate fusion between the *atman*, the individual soul, and Brahman, or God. But in the Buddha's teachings there is no need for a creator God, a prime mover, an ultimate supreme being to fuse with; on the contrary, it is through the forgetting of self and the

desire for union that reality is revealed: there is no need for a God in order for liberation to take place.

The Dharma cultivates the primacy of wisdom and compassion, discipline, humility, faith, devotion and obedience, and a transcendence of the fear of death.

All these virtues are found in other religions, but normally there is a belief in a deity. Buddhism's profound nontheistic nature is unimportant as far as practice is concerned because speculation regarding the existence of a supreme creator deity is irrelevant in the pursuit of liberation. In fact, strongly held mental concepts are fetters and obstructions. The Dharma teachings are verified by practice, and although the human mind sets up oppositions such as a belief in science versus revealed religion and a creator God, Buddhism is concerned with neither. The field of exploration for those who follow the Dharma is the world of inner realization, regardless of whether or not it is rational.

The idea that there are substantial existing and enduring *things* leads to attachment, which in turn leads to anger, greed, delusion, war, and enmity. Attachment, however, is not just to things but also to ideas and rituals; in particular, ideas of how we "ought to behave", and how things "should be". It extends to the defensive thought that I must not feel or think *this*, and I should and ought to feel or think *that*. Throughout history countless people have died because someone thinks that others should behave in a certain way or believe a particular thing.

Whether Perfect Ones appear in the world, or
whether Perfect Ones do not appear in the world,
it remains a condition, an immutable fact and
fixed law, that all formations are impermanent,
that all formations are subject to suffering, and
that everything is without a self.

FROM THE LAKKHANA-SUTTA
(ANGUTTARA NIKAYA)

The brilliant carriages of kings wear
out, and the body becomes old. But the
teachings of the wise never grow old;
they are passed on to the good.

THE DHAMMAPADA, VERSE 151
OF CHAPTER 11, OLD AGE

In the scenery of spring nothing is better,
nothing worse;
The flowering branches are;
some long, some short.

FROM THE ZENRINKUSHU BY EICHO (1429–1504)

Awaken the mind without fixing it anywhere.

FROM THE DIAMOND SUTRA

Impermanence

Human suffering arises from the property of impermanency, to which all existence is subject. By understanding impermanency, enlightenment is made possible.

> Impermanence is the rising, passing and changing of things, or the disappearance of things that have come into being or have arisen. This means that these things never persist in the same way, but are vanishing, changing, dissolving from moment to moment.
>
> FROM THE *VISUDDHIMAGGA* ("PATH TO PURITY")
> BY BUDDHAGOSA

It is due to impermanence that suffering, old age, sickness, and death arise. Because all phenomena are subject to change, even the most permanent-looking constituents of creation will eventually disappear. However, it is also due to impermanence that the solar system exists, that we are here and all that we know has come into being. The algorithm that underlies natural selection is based on the adaptation of existing forms. Without change there would be no evolution, and without evolved forms, no sentient beings; without sentient beings, no problems.

"The blind watchmaker" argument for gene-centric natural selection advocated by some zoologists is one that actually fits well with the Dharma view, which recognizes this *elan vital* as a great force. But given human ignorance (*avidya*) of the true nature of reality, humankind's in-built desire for food, shelter and reproduction, for recognition and pleasure, unless made fully conscious, will lead to serious consequences.

The solution is to become thoroughly familiar with impermanence in all its aspects, particularly that of the body, feelings, perception, habitual mental dispositions and consciousness, known as "the five aggregates" or *skandha*s (*khandha*s, P.). And to experience impermanence meditatively in the coming-to-be and ceasing-to-be of all phenomena. *Anicca-sanna* refers to the cognitive capacity to be able to say at all times "this is impermanence" and to know that "this is impermanence".

> Even if with a faithful heart we take refuge in the Triple Gem of the Buddha, the Teachings [Dharma] and the Community [Sangha], or develop a mind full of loving-kindness, it is far more meritorious if one cultivates the perception of impermanence even for a single moment.
>
> ANGUTTARA NIKAYA

Once impermanence has been thoroughly understood change can be enjoyed and we can "go with it" – every day is a new day:

> Sitting quietly doing nothing,
> Spring comes, grass grows of itself.
>
> FROM THE *ZENRINKUSHU* BY EICHO (1429–1504)

It Will Pass

This traditional story says something about the nature of time, impermanence and the importance of patience. It is said that the king truly understood the message concealed within the gold band, and was often seen looking inside his ring. Like waves in the ocean, both feelings and lives are transitory and last but a moment.

Once there was a great king and in his kingdom lived a great jeweller. So fine and artful was his work that it was rumoured the gods came to his workshop at night and secretly created his wares for him.

The king summoned the jeweller to the court and instructed him to make the very best piece of jewellery he could, no expense spared, because the king would present it to the queen. The monarch then waited and waited. At last, having lost patience, the king ordered the craftsman to appear and explain the delay. The man did so, saying very humbly that this work was the finest and most valuable he had ever begun – and could he have more time? The king reluctantly agreed, ordering him to return at the next full moon when without fail he was to present himself, this time with the finished piece.

The full moon duly came and the king waited expectantly, full of excitement at the prospect of seeing the work. Imagine his disappointment when all the jeweller presented him with was a simple gold band. Enraged, the king grasped his sword, ready to strike off the jeweller's head, when the desperate man said, "Wait my lord, look inside". The king did so. There, exquisitely set in precious stones, were the words "It will pass".

It is said the king understood the message, which gave him balance, and was delighted with the ring.

Suffering

The Pali word *dukkha* (suffering) has no decent equivalent in English. Translations of it have varied from "unsatisfactory" to "stress", as well as "liability to suffering", in the sense of "even good things come to an end". Enlightenment does not remove all suffering; the teachings of the Buddha serve as a guide to how to remove the suffering that arises as a consequence of the delusional beliefs in the existence of "I" and the concept of permanence.

Most important of all is the notion that no thing gives lasting satisfaction. If we accept that suffering is here to stay, life can get a lot easier. Enlightenment enables us to live with suffering and to understand truly what it is; suffering can even be a "friend", warning us of danger ahead. When we fully understand suffering in ourselves, we then grasp what its true function is and can act skilfully with it rather than fight against it. Fighting against suffering is in itself a form of suffering.

> Seeking satisfaction in the world, monks, I pursued my way. That satisfaction in the world, I found. In so far as satisfaction existed in the world, I have perceived it by wisdom. Seeking misery in the world, monks, I pursued my way. That misery in the world, I found. In so far as misery existed in the world, I have perceived it by wisdom. Seeking an escape from the world, monks, I pursued my way. That escape from the world, I found. In so far as an escape from the world existed, I have perceived it by wisdom.
>
> ANGUTTARA NIKAYA

"No-I"

If there is a single teaching that distinguishes Buddhism from all other religions and philosophical systems it is that there is no person, no being, no "my life", no entity, and no personality. There is no abiding fixed entity, no soul, no me, just this moment-to-moment perception. To believe in a person, a being, a life, an entity or a personality is to be deluded. The false belief in an individual self (*drshti/sakkaya-ditthi*) is the first of the "ten fetters". The others are doubt, attachment to rites and rituals, sensual desire, ill will, lusting for material existence, lusting for immaterial existence, conceit, restlessness and ignorance.

Personality belief became central to Mahayana doctrine, as is seen here in a passage from the Diamond Sutra, when the Buddha, in his teaching of the Great Way, delivered this homily:

> Every species of life, whether hatched in the egg, formed in the womb, evolved from spawn, produced by metamorphosis, with or without former intelligence, possessing or devoid of natural instinct – from these changeful conditions of being, I command you to seek deliverance in the transcendental concept of *nirvana*. Thus, you shall be delivered from an immeasurable, innumerable and illimitable world of sentient life from which we seek deliverance. And why? Because in the minds of enlightened disciples there have ceased to exist such arbitrary concepts of phenomena as an entity, a being, a living being, or a personality.
>
> THE DIAMOND SUTRA

"No-I" is probably the best way to describe complete-at-oneness-with-the-moment – for example, when we are completely absorbed in what we love. The opposite of this is feeling awkward or self-conscious, anxious or embarrassed. The "I" is clearly present when a person is in a state of anger over something. The loss of someone very dear is a time when anyone can be very conscious of this sense of "I", "me" and "mine".

The Buddhist point of view is that it is incorrect to attribute to various cognitive functions any existence as an entity. The Freudian term "ego" is not to be confused with the "I" of Buddhism. Ego is one element in a theory of how the human psyche is structured – from the Buddhist perspective, such a false illusion constitutes a form of attachment.

This was the teaching recorded in the Anattalakkhana Sutta, the Sermon on the Not-Self Characteristic. Given when the Buddha met up with his former companions after his enlightenment, during it he said:

> Body is not the self, feelings are not the self, perceptions and the activities of consciousness are not the self, therefore brethren every body whatever, be it past, present or future, be it inward, outward, gross or subtle, low or high, far or near, this is how it should be regarded: "This is not mine, this is not me, this is not myself."
>
> FROM THE ANATTALAKKHANA SUTTA
> (SAMYUTTA NIKAYA)

When we first seek the truth (the Dharma), we think we are far from it. When we discover that the truth is already in us, we are all at once our original self. If we watch the shore from a boat, it seems that the shore is moving. But when we watch the boat directly, we know it is the boat that is moving.

If we look at the world with a deluded body, and mind, we will think that our self is permanent. But if we practice correctly and return to our true self, we will realize that nothing is permanent.

FROM "*GENJOKOAN*": THE MANIFESTATION OF THE TRUTH IN *SHOBOGENZO* BY DOGEN (1200–1253)

The implications of "No-I" are profound because human beings waste so much time and energy trying to build up a sense of "me" and "mine". This sense, as psychologists will tell us, is usually a completely manufactured one that bears little resemblance to what someone is really like and is a source of pride and narcissistic self-love. People cling to pleasure, to strange ideas, and to rituals of all kinds, thinking these will take away their anxieties – but more than anything people hold on to the idea that they have some kind of permanent "I".

Kisa Gotami and the Mustard Seed

Once there lived in Savatthi a rich man's wife called Kisa Gotami, who gave birth to a beautiful little girl, to whom she naturally became very attached. One day the girl died suddenly and Kisa Gotami became distraught with grief. None of her family, friends or neighbours were able to do anything to comfort her, and she would not put down the dead child.

It so happened that the Buddha was passing near where she lived and, hearing this, Kisa Gotami ran to him, asking if there was anything he could possibly do to help to bring the child back to life? Instantly understanding the situation, the Buddha asked Kisa Gotami to fetch a mustard seed from a house in which no death had occurred.

In the Buddha's time every house had mustard seeds in the kitchen for cooking, so Kisa Gotami set off full of hope. At the first house she enquired: "Do you have a mustard seed? If you do and you give it to me, my daughter will be brought back to life by the Buddha."
There came the reply: "Yes, of course, we have a mustard seed. I will quickly fetch it so your daughter will be brought back to life again."

As the householder was about to hurry off, Kisa

Gotami called out: "Just one thing: no one must have died in this house."

The householder's face fell: "I am so sorry Kisa Gotami, my old mother died here only last year."

Undaunted, Kisa Gotami continued to the next house. By the evening she returned to the Buddha having been unable to find a single house in which no death had occurred. The Buddha's eyes were full of tears as he comforted her, and explained to her the nature of mortality. She was at last able to lay down the little body of her dead daughter, and in that laying down she was also able to throw off the load that we all carry – the burden of "I".

FROM THE THERIGATHA (KHUDDAKA NIKAYA)

It is said: "The living are few and the dead are many." But the Buddha's teachings bring hope, because to follow in the Buddha's footsteps is to meet the "deathless".

SAMYUTTA NIKAYA

Better to understand for a single day the fleeting nature of things than to live for a hundred years without such understanding.

Better a day with the vision of *nirvana* than a hundred years of blindness to the truth.

THE DHAMMAPADA – VERSES 113 AND 114
OF CHAPTER 8, "THE THOUSANDS"

The Three Fires

The doctrine of "dependent origination" (the chain of causation) and "the three signs of being" are universals, whereas the "three fires" of desire, anger and delusion (*trsna/lobha, raga/dosa, avidya/moha*) refer to individual human beings. They are sometimes called the "passions" or the "three poisons" (the "unwholesome roots" in the Southern Tradition). They are expressed and acted out by body (the things we do), by speech (the things we say), and by mind (the things we think). Each can only exist in the presence of a sense of "I", "me" or "mine". Walking the path of the Buddha is a way of transforming these fires. The Buddha's liberation, or enlightenment, took place when the sense of "I" dissolved – when all his fear had disappeared, he was no longer bound by the "three fires". People need to become aware of the three because they are the major source of suffering for ourselves and others. There is an unattributed saying from the Zen tradition: "The greater the passion, the greater the Buddha" – it is an acknowledgment of the fact that the passions are the root energy of transformation from which the *buddha*-nature grows.

In some religions these "fires" are repressed, called sins, and become the source of much anxiety, guilt and low self-esteem, punishable by eternal damnation. In Buddhism it is recognized that the fires are inevitably present for as long as there exists even the tiniest element of selfishness, self-consciousness or wilfulness. "Intentional action" is the term used to express all *karma*-producing actions. Intentionality, in this context, refers to the need to have things "my way" rather than "going with the flow", such as occurs spontaneously when the "I" is no longer dominant.

All schools of Buddhism concentrate on transforming this narrow selfishness. The way that these "fires" express themselves is through attachment – to reputation, job, status, and so on. People obtain a sense of who they are by identifying with something. The "fires" or "passions", being expressions of what it is to be human, can be tamed rather than repressed. When truly trained and gentled the energies of the passions can give rise to the noblest of human action and the best in human culture.

> I have conquered all things, I know all things, and I am free from them all. I have given up all and so I am freed by the destruction of craving. Whom can I call my teacher?
>
> THE DHAMMAPADA – VERSE 353
> OF CHAPTER 24, "THIRST"

> He is a *brahmin* who is a conqueror, a great sage, free from craving and an Enlightened One.
>
> THE DHAMMAPADA – VERSE 422
> OF CHAPTER 26, "THE BRAHMANA"

> There is no fire like hatred, no torrent like greed, and no snare like illusion.
>
> THE DHAMMAPADA – VERSE 251
> OF CHAPTER 18, "IMPURITY"

Dig out the root of craving as one digs up the birana grass to get the usira root. Do not let evil crush you as a flood crushes the reeds.

THE DHAMMAPADA – VERSE 337
OF CHAPTER 24, "THIRST"

The man who overcomes the fierce thirst of craving, suffering falls off from him like water drops from a lotus leaf.

THE DHAMMAPADA – VERSE 336
OF CHAPTER 24, "THIRST"

Let a man overcome hatred and pride and all fetters. He who does not cling to name or form, and who calls nothing his own, will not be destroyed by sorrow.

THE DHAMMAPADA – VERSE 221
OF CHAPTER 17, "ANGER"

Irrigators guide water; fletchers straighten arrows; carpenters bend wood; wise men shape themselves.

> THE DHAMMAPADA – VERSE 145
> OF CHAPTER 10, "PUNISHMENT"

As rust which springs from the iron destroys it, so the evil that men do destroys them.

> THE DHAMMAPADA – VERSE 240
> OF CHAPTER 18, "IMPURITY"

The gift of the Law [Dhamma] is greater than all other gifts; the taste of the Law [Dhamma] is sweeter than all other; love of the Law [Dhamma] exceeds all other love; the destruction of craving overcomes all suffering.

> THE DHAMMAPADA – VERSE 354
> OF CHAPTER 24, "THIRST"

. . . covetousness, ill-will, and wrong views – these things are due to either greed, hate or delusion.

> ANGUTTARA NIKAYA

> The antidote to lust is the perception of impurity, the antidote to hate is the cultivation of loving-kindness, the antidote to delusion is the cultivation of wisdom.
>
> ANGUTTARA NIKAYA

> Enraptured with lust (greed), enraged with hate, blinded by delusion, overwhelmed, with mind ensnared, man aims at his own ruin, at others' ruin, at the ruin of both, and he experiences mental pain and grief. He follows evil ways in deeds, words and thoughts. . . . He really knows neither his own welfare, nor the welfare of others, nor the welfare of both. These things make him blind and ignorant, hinder his knowledge, are painful, and do not lead him to peace.
>
> ANGUTTARA NIKAYA

Delusion is frequently called ignorance and is considered the most difficult root of all to dispel. Despite this it is not a prime cause – it too has its conditions that allow it to arise.

> You yourself must make the effort. *Buddha*s only point the way. Those who have entered the path and who meditate will be freed from the fetter of delusion.
>
> THE DHAMMAPADA – VERSE 276 OF CHAPTER 20, "THE WAY"

> . . . as long as we are human, we cannot escape from *karma* . . . for we are *karma*, and the latter

will follow us wherever we go, like our own shadow; but because of this we are able to escape from it; that is transcend it. Ordinarily, we are constantly under the oppressive consciousness of *karma*-bondage, and this fact we express in the spiritual urge to rise above ourselves or to approach God by perfecting or purifying ourselves, if that is possible.

FROM A LECTURE "THE ESSENCE OF BUDDHISM"
GIVEN BY DAISETZ TEITARO SUZUKI IN 1946

Those in search of the Way do not realize the existence and true nature of the self;
This is because they recognize only the relative mind,
Which is the origin of our eternal transmigration;
Foolish people take it for the true original self.

FROM THE *MUMONKAN* ("THE GATELESS GATE")
BY MUMON EKAI (1183–1260)

If you have attained the Way, all things are as though of one great family,
But if not, everything is separate and disconnected.
If you have not attained the Way all things are as of one family. [reality is unaffected]
And if you have attained the Way every single thing is different from every other thing.

FROM THE *MUMONKAN* ("THE GATELESS GATE")
BY MUMON EKAI (1183–1260)

The Fire Sermon

This sermon was the Buddha's third discourse, given to converted worshippers of sacred fire. Arguing that the ancient ritual was futile, the Buddha sought to replace it with something more meaningful. Their "sense bases" are burning with desire, anger and delusion, as are all mental phenomena arising from them; only when they are disillusioned with this infatuation will freedom be possible.

Thus, I heard. On one occasion the Blessed One was living at Gayasisa, together with a thousand monks. There he addressed them.

Monks, all is on fire. What is the "all" that is burning?

The eye is burning; forms seen are burning; consciousness of that seen by the eye is burning; contact with what the eye sees is burning; also, whatever is felt as a pleasant feeling, or painful or neutral feeling, that arises with eye-contact for its indispensable condition, that too is burning. Burning with what? Burning with the fire of lust,

with the fire of hate, with the fire of delusion.
I say it is burning with birth, ageing and death,
with sorrows, with lamentations, with pains,
with grief, with despair.

The ear is burning, sounds are burning . . .
The nose is burning, odours are burning . . .
The tongue is burning, flavours are burning . . .
The body is burning, tangibles are burning . . .

The mind is burning, ideas are burning, mind-
consciousness is burning, mind-contact is burning;
also, whatever is felt as pleasant, or painful or
neutral, that arises with mind-contact for its
indispensable condition, that too is burning.

Burning with what? Burning with the fire of lust,
with the fire of hate, with the fire of delusion.
I say it is burning with birth, ageing and death,
with sorrow, with lamentations, with pains, with
grief, with despair.

Monks, when a noble follower who has heard
(the truth) sees thus, he finds disenchantment
in the eye, finds disenchantment in forms, finds
disenchantment in eye-consciousness, finds
disenchantment in eye-contact; and whatever is
felt as pleasant, or painful or neutral, that arises
with eye-contact for its indispensable condition,
in that too he finds disenchantment.

He finds disenchantment in the ear . . . in sounds . . .
He finds disenchantment in the nose . . . in odours . . .
He finds disenchantment in the tongue . . . in flavours . . .
He finds disenchantment in the body . . . in tangibles . . .

He finds disenchantment in the mind, finds disenchantment in ideas, finds disenchantment in mind-consciousness, finds disenchantment in mind-contact; and whatever is felt as pleasant, or painful or neutral, that arises with mind-contact for its indispensable condition, in that too there is not seduction.

When he finds disenchantment, passion fades out. With the fading of passion, he is liberated. When liberated, the knowledge arises that he is liberated. He understands: "Birth is exhausted, the holy life has been lived out, what can be done is done, of this there is no more beyond."

That is what the Blessed One said. The monks were glad, and they approved his words. Now during his utterance, the hearts of those thousand monks were liberated from clinging no more

ADITTA SUTTA (SAMYUTTA NIKAYA)

Do Not Be Deceived

Because we are "on fire" with our own desires, we see what we wish to see. Our perceptions can reflect our preoccupations rather than reality. In this traditional tale from Tibet, the "fire" is ignorance, or blindness. The nomad has not come to terms with the loss of his father; his wife is jealous, thus sees a rival; while the old woman sees herself, without knowing it.

A simple nomad lived on a mountain with his wife and mother-in-law. Both his parents were dead. One day he had to go to the town for provisions. He came to a shop that sold, among other things, mirrors, and never having seen one before, he looked into it and saw what appeared to be the image of his long-dead father. He rushed into the shop and bought it, before concealing it in his bag in the belief that it was magical. Once safely back at home, every night he would take the mirror from the bag and look at what he thought was his father. His wife saw him doing this and began to wonder what it was he was concealing from her, and while he was out attending to the herds she searched through his bag until she found the mirror. Staring into it she saw a beautiful young woman and immediately shouted: "That rascally husband of mine has a new girlfriend." Her mother said: "Hand it to me, I'm sure I'll know who it is." Picking up the mirror, she looked into it and exclaimed: "Are you mad? Why, this is a picture of an old hag, you have nothing to fear."

The Middle Path

The Middle Path (*madhyama-pratipad* S., *majjhima-patipada* P.), or Middle Way, was the first teaching given by the Buddha after his enlightenment. He delivered it to his five disciples who had previously abandoned him on account of his supposed self-indulgence. Preceding The Four Noble Truths and The Noble Eightfold Path, the teaching is part of the *sutra* known as the "Turning of the Wheel" (the Dhammacakkappavattana Sutta in the Samyutta Nikaya). This single passage has had the most influence on the evolution of Buddhism, from its earliest doctrinal beginnings to the most highly developed of the Mahayana Schools, and summarizes all subsequent doctrinal development.

To give oneself up to indulgence in sensual pleasure, the base, common, vulgar, unholy, unprofitable; and also to give oneself up to self-torment, the painful, unholy, unprofitable: both these two extremes the Perfect One has avoided and found the Middle Path, which causes one both to see and to know, which leads to peace, to discernment, to enlightenment, to *nirvana*.

It is the Noble Eightfold Path, the way that leads to the extinction of suffering, namely: right view [understanding], right thought, right speech, right bodily action, right livelihood, right effort, right mindfulness [awareness], and right concentration.

SAMYUTTA NIKAYA

The Buddha was cautioning the monks against the adoption of extreme positions – to avoid pursuing sensual indulgence just as much as ruthless self-deprivation or asceticism. Nevertheless, one should embrace life in all its complexity and live it to the full and unequivocally, yet do so without being engulfed by it. The correct path to follow was a middle way between materialism and nihilism. Between longing and craving on the one side and aversion and loathing on the other, there is emptiness. This empty, indescribable state – of complete emotional calm – is *sunyata*, or voidness.

In the second century CE an interpretative tradition known as the School of the Middle Way, or Madhyamika, was founded by Nagarjuna, who was to have an important influence on the development of Mahayana Buddhism. A key doctrine of Nagarjuna was the "Two Truths" – relative truth, the everyday reality of me/you and things having separate existence, and the absolute truth of *nirvana*.

The Madhyamika stresses that the mind is pure and unblemished, empty of any defilements, which are like clouds obscuring the sun. Once the clouds have lifted, reality appears – but the sun was always there from the outset. A later development of Madhyamika called Yogachara ("Practice of Yoga") states that there are in fact three truths and that consciousness is the ultimate reality.

In the Dharma there are no distinctions;
These arise only from clinging to this or that.
The heart itself creates its delusions,
Is this not the greatest of all mistakes?
In delusion are notions of rest and motion,
Awakened, there is neither liking nor loathing.
All pairs of opposites
Are the product of our own folly.
Dreams, delusions, flowers in the empty air,
Why trouble to lay hold of them?

> FROM THE *HSIN-HSIN MING* ('ON FAITH IN
> THE HEART') ATTRIBUTED TO SOSAN
> (CHAN PATRIARCH; DIED 606)

He is a *brahmin* who has given up
both pleasure and pain, become calm
and energetic and has overcome all worlds.

> THE DHAMMAPADA – VERSE 418 OF CHAPTER 26,
> 'THE BRAHMANA'

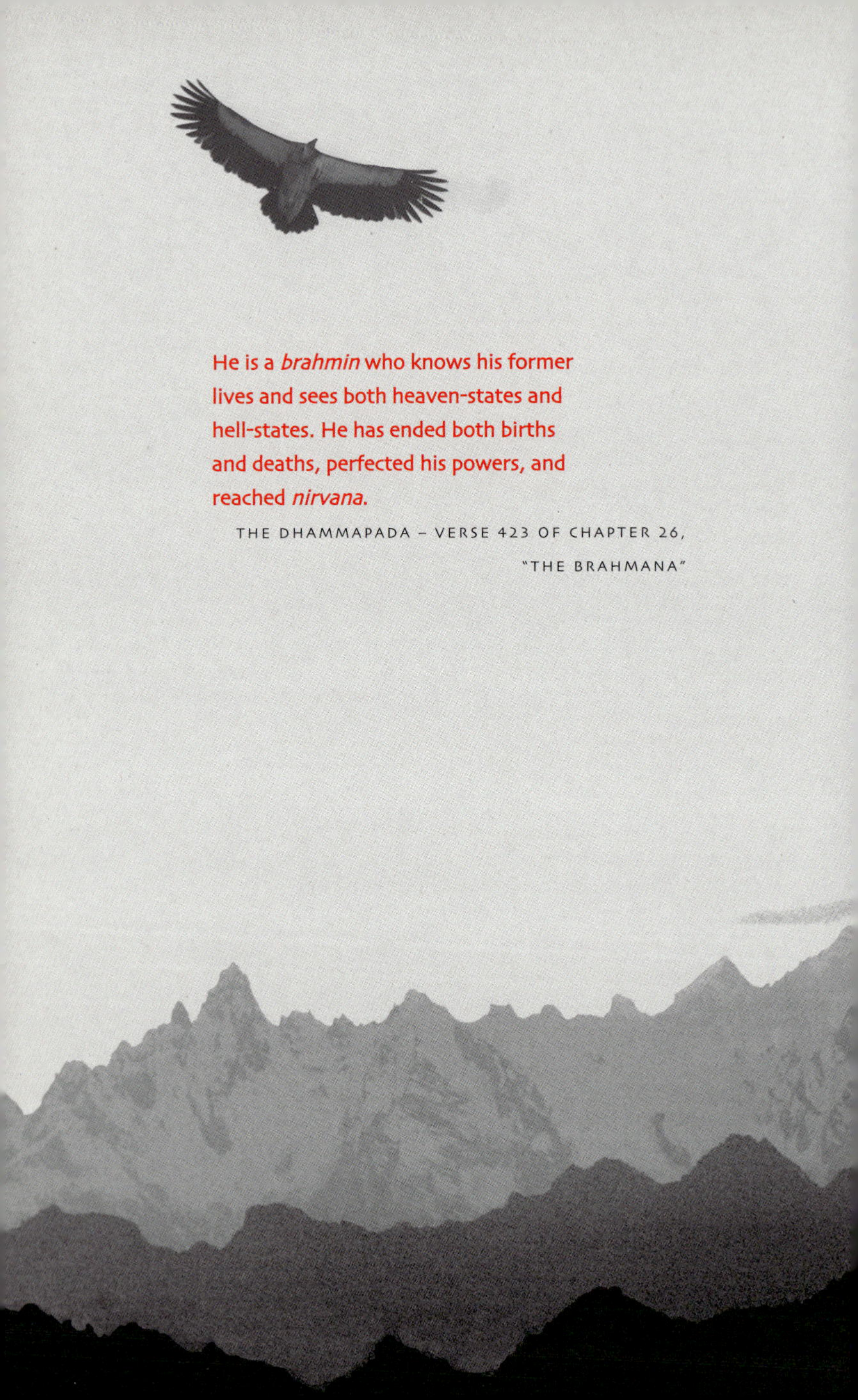

He is a *brahmin* who knows his former lives and sees both heaven-states and hell-states. He has ended both births and deaths, perfected his powers, and reached *nirvana*.

THE DHAMMAPADA – VERSE 423 OF CHAPTER 26,
"THE BRAHMANA"

The Great Way is not difficult, it only avoids
picking and choosing.

> FROM THE *HSIN HSIN MING* ("ON FAITH IN
> THE HEART") ATTRIBUTED TO SOSAN
> (CHAN PATRIARCH, DIED 606)

The Four Noble Truths

There is nowhere where there is no birth, no ageing, no decay, no rebirth; nevertheless, I do not say an end of suffering cannot be made. For it can be ended here and now.

ANGUTTARA NIKAYA

During the Buddha's first sermon (see page 99) he uttered the Four Noble Truths (*ariya sacca*, P.), which provide his most enduring formulation of doctrine, diagnosing the human condition and prescribing a treatment. He stated that suffering exists; there is a cause for suffering; the cause is desire or craving; and the end to suffering is the Noble Eightfold Path. These simple statements are "noble"

because they can confer true nobility on the practitioner through moral action rather than through the accident of birth. In the Buddha's time India was stratified into four social classes, or *varnas*, which a person was born into. A priestly class of Brahmans at the top, above a warrior class of Kshatriyas, a mercantile class of Vaishyas, and a worker-servant class of Shudras. The Buddha understood nobility in a different way, as being a moral state – something that could be earned in one's own life, just as *arhat*ship could be.

The Buddha's own enlightenment arose through his realization of these truths. In making the statements, the Buddha's only concern was the removal of human suffering (or unsatisfactoriness, *duhkha/dukkha*). The Four Noble Truths refer not to all suffering but only to that which it is possible to remove – the suffering that arises from desire.

The First Sermon

Derived from the example of the Four Noble Truths is the epithet "the great physician" that is sometimes given to the Buddha. This is because he looked at the symptoms, in this case the suffering of humanity, and then identified the cause as desire. What every physician does is prescribe a treatment: the steps that need to be taken to overcome the illness and reach a state of health – and in this case the cure is the Noble Eightfold Path. In the Mahayana tradition this aspect of the Buddha became the Great Medicine Buddha, always depicted as blue and associated with lapis lazuli, the blue semi-precious stone that is flecked with gold.

It was at the Deer Park in Benares that the Buddha declaimed the Four Noble Truths to his disciples during what has become known as "The First Sermon":

... Now this, brethren, is the truth about suffering: Birth is suffering, decay is suffering, sickness is suffering, death is suffering, likewise sorrow and grief, woe, lamentation and despair. To be conjoined with things which we dislike, to be separated from things which we like – that also is suffering. Not to get what one wants – that also is suffering. In a word, this body, this fivefold mass which is based on grasping, that is suffering.

Now this, brethren, is the truth about the origin of suffering: It is that craving that leads downwards to birth, along with the lure and the lust that lingers longingly, now here, now there; namely, the craving for sensation, the craving to be born again, the craving to have done with rebirth. Such, brethren, is the truth about the origin of suffering.

And this, brethren, is the truth about the ceasing of suffering: Truly, it is the utter passionless cessation of, the giving up, the forsaking, the release from, the absence of longing for, this craving.

Now this, brethren, is the truth about the way leading to the ceasing of suffering. Truly, it is this Eightfold Path, that is: Right view, right thought, right speech, right action, right livelihood, right effort, right mindfulness and right concentration.

SAMYUTTA NIKAYA

The First Noble Truth

This is one of the "three signs of being" – that suffering, hardship and unsatisfactoriness is the lot of humankind. It does not deny happiness or pleasure and life's simple joys, but argues that they too come to an end and are therefore transient and passing.

The Buddha likened pleasure to "licking honey from a knife" – sooner or later we will get hurt by it; it is not that there is anything wrong with pleasure, but the compulsive pursuit of it leads to unhappiness. Even if we are sat comfortably and all seems well, in no time at all we have to move and find a new position.

To probe a little deeper, something inside human beings is restless and unsatisfied and craves now for "this" and now for "that". Nothing seems to be enough. As Pascal said, all the troubles in the world arise because man is unable to sit quietly alone in a room.

The Second Noble Truth

If we cannot find a cause for an illness then we will not be able to find a cure, but once we know that there is a source then something can at least be done. Understanding the twelve-linked chain of causation and the nature of causality, we can see that the factors giving rise to suffering can be interrupted. Craving and desire and grasping can be stopped. Attachment underlies all removable human suffering. In the Buddhist texts there are three different forms of desire according to the object longed for.

The word for desire is *tanha*, which can be translated as thirst, craving or desire. The scorching heat of summer in India made thirst a tangible fear for people and would have been understood immediately by the Buddha's audience.

The first object of desire is pleasure, the intense craving for physical satisfaction of one sort or another, be it dietary or carnal. The second object of desire is to *be* someone, the boss, famous, some kind of celebrity – important in some way; the absolute craving for being. The third is the desire for oblivion, for annihilation – suicide to avoid the challenge of life, or to avoid the challenges of existence by losing oneself in drugs or alcohol.

Attachment is another way of looking at the cause and one often used in the texts. The sense of entitlement, for example, that many of us carry quite unconsciously, that arises when we are thwarted in some way – poor service in a restaurant, waiting for delayed transport, losing out in love.

Sometimes we feel that we are awful people. Unconsciously we carry a sense of low self-esteem, guilt and depression, and we feel we are failures in life, undeserving of the ordinary dignities that are natural. This gives rise to an avoidant way of life, and is a form of desire.

The conditions that give rise to ailments which psychiatrists, analysts and psychotherapists are used to encountering all come under this noble truth.

The Third Noble Truth

The third truth states that we can give up that craving or desire, but first it must be identified. Most people think their situation is normal and does not require any kind of investigation, thus they go through life suffering, unaware that anything can be done about it. Once people become aware – which essentially is what the practice of Buddhism is concerned with – then they are in a position to do something, letting go of all the false dreams that they hold so dear, those unrealistic desires and fierce passions.

The Fourth Noble Truth
By following the Noble Eightfold Path (see pages 106–113) deliverance is possible.

Thinking for Yourself

The Buddha was at pains to point out that if, by experiment, his "medication" was effective then it should be taken up, and if it wasn't then it should be forgotten. He emphasized the importance of individual practice and experimentation in liberating people from their conditioned states.

The importance of finding out for oneself is a teaching that is set out in the Kalama Sutta. The Buddha admonishes his audience against doing something just because someone says so. Nor should people follow a teaching because it issues from authority, for which we can only assume that the Buddha was thinking of the established authority and traditions of the time, including the Vedic. Also, something shouldn't be done purely because it seems reasonable. In the passage, the Buddha discounts one by one the various reasons why we might consider taking up a particular belief or a practice.

The Kalama Sutta goes on to state that if a teaching is practised and found to be effective then it needs to be taken up. Applied to the mind, in the history of ideas this is significant because it is the scientific method in practice: presented in a forthright way, using experimentation and reliant not upon any higher authority than the evidence of one's own senses.

Then the Kalamas of Kesaputta came to the exalted one and said: "*Lord, there are here some recluses and* brahmins *who come to Kesaputta. They extol and magnify their own view, but the view of others they spitefully abuse, depreciate, pluck it bare.* [lit. pull out its feathers.] *Then, Lord, other recluses and* brahmins *come to Kesaputta . . . and do the same. And as we listen to them, doubt and wavering arise in us as to which of the parties is telling the truth and which of the parties is telling lies.*"

Well may you doubt, Kalamas; well may you waver; for your wavering arises about a matter that is open to doubt.

Now, Kalamas, do not go by hearsay, nor by what is handed down by others, nor by what people say, nor by what is stated on authority of your traditional teachings. Do not go by reasoning, nor by inferring, nor by argument as to method, nor from reflection on and approval of an opinion, nor out of respect, thinking a recluse must be deferred to. But, Kalamas, when you know of yourselves: "These teachings are not good; they are blameworthy; they are condemned by the wise: these teachings, when followed through and put into practice, help to bring about loss and suffering" – then reject them.

FROM THE KALAMA SUTTA
(IN THE ANGUTTARA NIKAYA)

The Noble Eightfold Path

The eight elements of the Noble Eightfold Path (*ariya-atthangika-magga*, P.) are traditionally arranged into three groups. Morality (*shila* S./*sila* P.) comprises right speech, right bodily action and right livelihood or living. Concentration or meditation (*samadhi* P.) comprises right effort, right mindfulness or awareness and right concentration. Wisdom (*prajna* S./*panna* P.) comprises right view and right thought (the "right" connotes a skilful or appropriate, rather than perfect, form).

The Buddha emphasized the path as a practical way of living, and although the path leads to emancipation it is a guide for how to live in the here and now rather than one that encourages its user to look ahead for a reward, setting up a virtuous circle that builds on itself. Although eightfold, the path is indivisible and all of one piece – like a single cloth with eight folds.

The two wisdom elements refer to understanding the causes of suffering, and this understanding deepens as the practice proceeds. The morality elements are a prerequisite for meditation and the development of concentrated awareness, which in turn deepens at oneness-with-the-moment, leading to a more profound understanding of the Four Noble Truths. And so on. The path is the way that leads out of suffering and during his first sermon the Buddha described it to his five companions:

> Now what, brethren is right view?
> The knowledge about ill, the arising of ill, the ceasing of ill, and the way leading to the ceasing of ill – that, brethren, is called right view.

And what, brethren is right aim? [thought] The being set on renunciation, on non-resentment, on harmlessness – that, brethren, is called right aim.

And what, brethren, is right speech? Abstinence from lying speech, from backbiting and abusive speech, and from idle babble – that, brethren, is called right speech.

And what, brethren, is right action? Abstinence from taking life, from taking what is not given, from wrongdoing in sexual passions – that, brethren, is called right action.

And what, brethren, is right living? Herein, brethren, the . . . disciple, by giving up wrong living, gets his livelihood by right living – that, brethren, is right living.

And what, brethren is right effort? Herein, brethren, a brother generates the will to inhibit the arising of evil immoral conditions that have not yet arisen; he makes an effort, he sets energy afoot, he applies his mind and struggles. Likewise (he does the same) to reject evil immoral conditions that have already arisen. Likewise (he does the same) to reject evil immoral conditions that have not yet arisen. Likewise (he does the same) to cause the arising of good conditions that have not already arisen. Likewise he does the same to establish, to prevent corruption, to cause the increase, the practice, the fulfilment

> of conditions that have already arisen. This, brethren, is called right effort.
>
> And what, brethren, is called right mindfulness? Herein, brethren, a brother dwells regarding body as compound, he dwells ardent, self-possessed, recollected, by controlling the covetousness and dejection that are in the world. So also with regard to feelings, with regard to perception, with regard to activities . . . with regard to thought. This brethren, is called right mindfulness [awareness]. . . .
>
> DIGHA NIKAYA

The Noble Eightfold Path is an attempt to make each of us conscious of all the things that we do and think based on our understanding of the teachings at a given time. For example, in respect of "right livelihood/living", there are professions that are considered unwholesome, such as working in slaughterhouses or selling armaments; however, a person making a living by selling things may feel that is a perfectly honourable thing to do. After some years of immersion in the Buddha's teachings that same person may decide that because his or her mind is preoccupied with profit and loss, they would rather do something else that was better suited to their revised perception of the teaching. In this sense, laypeople find that the path contains considerable room for interpretation and development. For those in a monastic environment life is quite different; there, all actions are entirely devoted to the Buddha Dharma, and all things are "Buddha things" carried out wholeheartedly for the sake of the Buddha Dharma.

We may think we do not meditate but we do. Whenever something is important to us we become absorbed in it to the exclusion of all else. One-pointed concentration is, in fact, a natural function, but what practising it does is alter it into something that can be of great benefit. A person struggling with substance dependency can show great concentration-energy and absorption but the result is detrimental; if the object is changed, the outcome will become very different.

So, gradually, step by step, the further

the practice progresses the greater the insight, and slowly the landscape transforms as changes are made.

> Putting away pleasure and possessing nothing of his own, the wise man will cleanse himself from every evil thought.
> THE DHAMMAPADA – VERSE 88 OF CHAPTER 6, "THE WISE MAN"

Although social and personal circumstances will play their part in contributing to how an individual suffers, in Buddhist thought blame is seen as a "poison" that will only lead to negative actions and will do nothing to reduce suffering.

Better than a thousand senseless verses is one which brings the hearer peace.

Better than a thousand useless verses is one word of the law which brings the hearer peace.

Though one man conquer a thousand times a thousand men in battle, he who conquers himself is the greatest warrior.

THE DHAMMAPADA – VERSES 101–103
OF CHAPTER 8, "THE THOUSANDS"

The Paramitas

There are ten moral or mental qualities that, when perfectly realized, lead to *buddha*-hood. Called *paramitas*, these "perfections", as they are also known, play a larger role in Mahayana traditions, as part of the development of the *bodhisattva* ideal. Mahayana followers recognize six: giving (*dana*), morality or proper conduct (*sila*), patience (*khanti*), energy or vigour (*viriya*), meditation (*dhyana*) and wisdom (*panna*). Theravada followers recognize ten, the *dasa paramiyo*: giving (*dana*), morality or proper conduct (*sila*), renunciation (*nekkhama*), wisdom (*panna*), energy or vigour (*viriya*), patience (*khanti*), truthfulness (*sacca*), resolution or resolve (*adhitthana*), loving-kindness (*metta*) and equanimity (*upekkha*).

Giving (*dana*)

Giving is the cultivation of a particular frame of mind that counteracts natural selfishness and desire. It extends from the giving of alms, both to those less fortunate than ourselves and to support the community of monastics, to all acts of liberality and generosity – the giving of oneself.

> Five blessings accrue to the giver of alms: the affection of many, noble association, good reputation, self-confidence, and heavenly rebirth.
>
> ANGUTTARA NIKAYA

Ultimately we need to give up all thoughts of and attachment to self – this is the purpose of the Theravada mental quality of renunciation. To attain the non-duality of *samadhi*, it is necessary to give every fibre of our being

to whatever we are doing, moment to moment. If we are interested in what we are doing, we accomplish this anyway – reading an enjoyable book is a good example of how easy absorption can be. A problem arises when an activity does not interest us, which is when we need to know how to "give ourselves to" what we are doing – but this can be cultivated and it forms the basis of all genuine practice.

Morality (sila)

Sometimes called virtue, *sila* implies the idea of sustained restraint. It is one of the "three types of training", alongside concentration and wisdom. In the Noble Eightfold Path (see page 106) there are three moral ideals – right speech, right action and right livelihood. These were later expanded into the moral code of early Buddhism known as the "Five Precepts" – general rules governing acceptable behaviour and applicable to everyone. No intentional destruction of life. No stealing. No sexual misconduct. No lying. No intoxication.

> He is a *brahmin* from whom pleasures drop like the water from a lotus, or mustard seed from the point of a needle.
>
> THE DHAMMAPADA – VERSE 401 OF CHAPTER 26, "THE BRAHMANA"

This cultivation of good conduct has other important benefits. For example, if we are trying to give up smoking we will be aware of our desire to have a cigarette – by exercising restraint we conquer desire. However, we have to be constantly aware to be wholly conscious of the signs that the physical desire is building. This constitutes good form – the alert, fully conscious "being in the moment".

The old-fashioned idea of a gentleman was someone who behaved well under all circumstances. To train oneself in virtue or morality is to forge a calm, steady state of relaxed-yet-alert vigilance – a solid platform for the cultivation of the heart and mind through more formal meditative practices.

> He is a *brahmin* who is free of fetters and without desires for this or any other world.
>
> THE DHAMMAPADA – VERSE 410 OF CHAPTER 26,
> "THE BRAHMANA"

Patience (*khanti*)

Sometimes called forbearance, *khanti* essentially means enduring the unendurable and tolerating the intolerable. This is a good practice for laypeople who, in their demanding lives, frequently find themselves with little time yet under pressure to get things done – a toxic brew. How often do we hear mothers screaming at their children, or harsh, curt responses to simple requests? This *paramita* is said to be a means to overcome anger (one of the hindrances to meditation), and to calm the passions of those with fiery temperaments.

> He is a *brahmin* who is content with a simple life and has few wants. He is neither a householder nor a beggar.
>
> THE DHAMMAPADA – VERSE 404 OF CHAPTER 26,
> "THE BRAHMANA"

> The fool thinks he has won a battle when he bullies with harsh speech, but only knowing how to be forbearing makes us victorious.
>
> SAMYUTTA NIKAYA

Vigour (*viraya*)

A fear that we may not get what we want can lead to people becoming unwilling to rise to life's challenges. Energy counteracts this fear and encourages people to abandon their procrastination and avoidance.

> By rousing himself . . . the wise man may make for himself an island which no flood can overwhelm.
>
> THE DHAMMAPADA – VERSE 25 OF CHAPTER 2, "ON EARNESTNESS"

Wisdom (*panna*)

With wisdom we can see the true nature of things, uncontaminated by personal bias. Wisdom is of three kinds: that attained through thinking, for example deductive reasoning; that acquired through learning; and that derived from higher mental development. This third form of wisdom is that which perceives the nature of reality, of suffering, impermanence and the insubstantiality of self. Thought, speech and action that arise from this state of mind is skilful and selfless. Wisdom confers the ability to understand what is and is not beneficial to human beings.

> Just as when a lamp is lit in a darkened room, a thousand years of darkness

immediately vanish, in the same way when the lamp of the Buddha's mind illuminates sentient beings, eons of darkness are immediately dispelled.

THE AVATAMSAKA SUTRA

(THE FLOWER GARLAND SUTRA)

All the *buddha*s of the past, present and future, after approaching the *paramita* of wisdom, have awoken to the highest knowledge.

THE HEART SUTRA

Renunciation (*nekkhama*)

The Buddha gave up everything to pursue his quest, yet he admitted that before he became enlightened his heart did not delight in the thought of giving up worldly pleasures. He realized, eventually, that he had not yet experienced life without them. By reducing the pull that sensual experiences have on us, we will attain freedom and real joy. Even doing without small things is meritorious; it cultivates strength.

He is a *brahmin* who is free of all human ties and all heavenly ties.

THE DHAMMAPADA – VERSE 417 OF CHAPTER 26,

"THE BRAHMANA"

Be content with simple things and free from the craving for worldly possessions.

TRADITIONAL TIBETAN

Surrendering everything is *nirvana*, and my mind seeks *nirvana*.

FROM THE *BODHICARYAVATARA* BY SHANTIDEVA

Truthfulness (*sacca*)

In the sense of doing what you say you will do, truthfulness may be the most important virtue because it is based on trust between people. In terms of the path, it means following it courageously to the end just as the Buddha did.

> Deceptions cease in the realm of truth. There are no boundaries to be seen.
>
> FROM THE *HSIN HSIN MING* ("ON FAITH IN THE HEART") ATTRIBUTED TO SOSAN (CHAN PATRIARCH, DIED 606)

Resolution (*adhitthana*)

Unshakeable resolution is needed to remain on the path, overcoming the difficulties that will arise. Attaining any goal requires determination and perseverance.

> It is good to apply yourself diligently to the task in hand. Intoxicated by that task, you should be completely focused, like someone striving to win a game.
>
> FROM THE *BODHICARYAVATARA* BY SHANTIDEVA

Loving-kindness (*metta*)

Considered an innate quality of the heart, loving-kindness has to be released from the fetters of fear and anxiety.

> Just as . . . at time of daybreak the star of healing shines and burns and flashes forth, even so, whatsoever grounds there be for good works undertaken with a view to rebirth, all of them are not worth one tiny part of that goodwill which is

the heart's release. Goodwill which is the heart's
release, alone shines and burns and flashes forth
in surpassing them.

THE UDANA (IN THE KHUDDAKA NIKAYA)

Equanimity (*upekkha*)

Meaning imperturbability, this is one of the sublime states
or *brahma-vihara*s (see page 131) that mark the advance
towards enlightenment. When the "I" is vanquished there is
no fear and all action arises from a state of equanimity, fully
aware and fully present.

A monk, by getting rid of anguish, through
diminishing his former pleasures and sorrows,
enters and abides in the fourth meditation, which
has neither anguish nor happiness and which is
entirely purified by equanimity and mindfulness.
This, Ananda, is the other happiness, which
is more excellent and exquisite than worldly
happiness.

MAJJHIMA NIKAYA

Meditation (*dhyana*)

Full, whole-hearted, single-minded attention to and mental
engrossment in whatever one is doing, is an essential
practice – not just in formal meditation, but at all times.

Without knowledge there is no meditation;
without meditation there is no knowledge. He
who has knowledge and meditation nears *nirvana*.

THE DHAMMAPADA – VERSE 372 OF CHAPTER 25,

"THE BHIKKHU"

The wish for betterment

The literal translation of *paramita* is "gone beyond" – beyond the selfish desires, blind instinctual drives and bad habits that constitute a typical person. As mentioned, "perfection" is the most commonly used translation but this has connotations of "perfectionism" and is suggestive of excessive piety and holiness, which misrepresents the whole spirit of the practice. Virtue may offer the best alternative, suggesting behaviour devoid of low, grasping intention,

that is skilful and appropriate at all times, and, most importantly, that is natural in the sense of innocent of ulterior, selfish motivation, and which implies strength.

It is a "state of mind" that is beyond grasping if one *paramita* is present so are the rest – with desire, anger or delusion no longer present, the sense of selfishness has gone. However, if it is a state of mind, then is it true that to behave generously when we do not feel generous is hypocritical? To go against our natural inclinations when it comes to spiritual practice can be a good thing, because that is when the work of transformation takes place – most spiritual paths have self-sacrifice at their centre, the sacrifice of that innate momentum – the ignorance – that keeps us blinkered and "unconscious". Despite the natural tendency to inertia on the part of many, others seek to realize their potential to the fullest extent and thereby help to propel a perfectly natural movement toward enlightenment. The teachings of the Buddha understand this wish for betterment, or *boddhicitta* as it is called in the Mahayana school. In "The Parable of the Log" (see pages 124–127) the Buddha illustrated the hazards that exist along the path of practice.

The parable indicates that in the absence of any inner obstructions, *nirvana* is inevitable – but because we do have attachments, which are impediments, then the cultivation of the *paramita*s will be of great help. Even the most circumspect person is likely to slip up every now and again. With such skilful means as the *paramita*s we can avoid the various snags of life – the "shoals" and "banks" – that will lead to disaster.

The Parable of the Log

Once the Exalted One was staying at Kosambi, on the bank of the River Ganges. When he saw a great log being carried down Ganges' stream, he called to the brethren, asking whether they could see the great log being carried downstream.

"*Yes Lord*", they replied.

Now, brethren, if a log does not ground on this bank or the further bank, if it does not sink in midstream, if it does not stick fast on a shoal, if it does not fall into human or non-human hands, if it is not caught on an eddy, or if it does not rot inwardly – that log, brethren, will float down to the ocean, will slide down to the ocean, will tend towards the ocean. And why? Because brethren, Ganges' stream floats down to the ocean, tends towards the ocean.

In like manner, brethren, if you do not ground on this shore or that shore, if you do not sink in midstream, if you do not stick fast on a shoal, if you do not fall prey to beings human and non-human, if you do not get caught in an eddy, if you do not rot inwardly – then, brethren, you shall float down to *nirvana*, you shall slide down to *nirvana*, you shall tend towards *nirvana*. And why? Because, brethren, perfect-view floats, slides, tends towards *nirvana*.

"What, Lord, is 'this bank', what is the 'other bank', what is 'sinking in midstream'? What is 'sticking fast on a shoal'? What is 'falling prey to beings human and non-human'? What is 'being caught in an eddy'? What is 'rotting inwardly'?"

"This bank", brother, is a name for the six personal spheres of sense-action. "That bank", brother, is a name for the six external spheres of sense-action.

"Sinking in midstream" is a name for lure and lust.

"Sticking fast on a shoal" is for the conceit of self.

And what, brother, is "being caught by humans"? In this matter, brother, a householder lives in society, rejoices with those who rejoice, sorrows with those who sorrow, takes pleasure with those who take pleasure, suffers with those who suffer, makes links with all manner of business that befalls. This, brother, is "being caught by humans".

And what brother is "being caught by non-humans"? In this matter, brother, such and such a brother lives the holy life with the wish to be reborn in the company of some class of *deva*s, with the thought: "May I by virtue or by practice or by some austerity or holy living become a *deva* or one of the *devas*." This, brother, is "being caught by non-humans". "Being caught in an eddy", brother, is a name for the pleasures of the five senses.

And what, brother is "rotting inwardly"? Herein, brother, a certain one is immoral, an evil-doer, impure, of suspicious behaviour, of covert deeds: he is no recluse, though recluse in vows; no liver of the holy life, though thereto: rotten within and full of lusts, he is a son of filth. Such, brother, is "rotting inwardly".

SAMYUTTA NIKAYA

The Way of Selfless Compassion

> My faults are innumerable. I vow to throw them all off. Sentient beings are innumerable. I vow to liberate them all. The teachings of the Buddha are innumerable. I vow to learn them all. The Way of the Buddha is unsurpassable. I vow to walk it to the end.
>
> THE FOUR VOWS (RECITED IN ZEN TEMPLES)

The *paramita*s are of great importance in Mahayana Buddhism. This occurred following a division in the early Buddhist community (ca. 200BCE) when two distinct camps emerged, though not in opposition to each other. One group inclined towards the *arhat* path, rooted in the teachings of the Buddha and an introspective analysis of phenomena, as laid out in the third book of the Sutta Pitaka (the Samyutta Nikaya). In the other group were those who wished to reach out towards others and who criticized the *arhat* path as a self-centred one in which individuals become absorbed with their own liberation to the detriment of the suffering of others around them. Eventually this was reflected in the Mahayana school's path of the *bodhisattva*, which emphasizes the development of wisdom and the cultivation of compassion towards others – only through such a selfless commitment can *buddha*-hood be realized.

The ideal of the *bodhisattva* was examined by the Indian monk Vasubandhu (ca.290–370CE) in the Abhidarmakosa ("Treasury of Metaphysics"), a complex analytical text about the nature of mind. A member of the orthodox Sarvastivada school, his mystical ideas led to the development of the Yogachara school and contributed to esoteric Buddhism.

But why do the bodhisattvas, once they have taken the vow to obtain supreme enlightenment, take such a long time to obtain it?

Because the supreme enlightenment is very difficult to obtain: one needs a vast accumulation of knowledge and merit, innumerable heroic deeds in the course of three innumerable *kalpa*s.

One could understand that bodhisattvas seek this enlightenment (so difficult to obtain) if this were the only means of enlightenment. But this is not the case. Why then do they undertake such infinite labour?

For the good of others, because they want to become capable of pulling others out of this great flood of suffering.

But what personal benefit do they find in the benefit of others?

The benefit of others is their own benefit, because they desire it.

Who could believe that?

It is true that men devoid of pity, and who think only of themselves, find it hard to believe in the altruism of the *bodhisattva*. But compassionate men do so easily.

> Do we not see that certain people, confirmed in
> the absence of pity, find pleasure in the suffering
> of others, even when it is not useful to them?
> As well, one must admit that the *bodhisattva*s,
> confirmed in pity, find pleasure in doing good to
> others without any egoistic preoccupation.
>
> Do we not see that certain people, ignorant of
> that true nature of the conditioned *dharma*s
> which constitute their so-called "self", attach
> themselves to these *dharmas* by force of habit
> – however completely these *dharmas* may be
> devoid of personality – and suffer a thousand
> pains because of this attachment?
>
> Likewise, one must admit that the *bodhisattva*s,
> by the force of habit, detach themselves from the
> *dharma*s which constitute the so-called "self", do
> no longer consider these *dharma*s as "I"or "mine",
> growing in pitying solicitude for others, and are
> ready to suffer a thousand pains for this solicitude.
>
> FROM THE ABHIDHARMAKOSA

None of this is to say that the Theravada tradition does not value the *paramita*s; quite the contrary: they provide an indispensable tool with which to deal with humankind's deeply seated propensity for pleasure, existence, pernicious views, and so on – destructive traits known as *asavas*.

The immediate antidote to the negative mental habit patterns represented by the *asava*s are four sublime states known as the *brahma-vihara*s, namely loving-kindness, compassion, altruistic joy (or being joyful at the joy of others – sympathetic joy), and equanimity.

Cultivation of the Heart

All Buddhists follow in the footsteps of one who attained full development as a man – The Thus Come, the Buddha. It is hard to know what the enlightened Buddha was actually like, but his way is continued through the legacy of his teachings – such as we have from the various schools and the global community of monastics and lay men and women – which offer people a means of cultivating the heart (meaning our centre of experience, or our seat of consciousness as Buddhaghosa referred to it) in order to develop themselves as a complete human being.

As well as referring to a historical figure, *buddha* is an active principal within – one which becomes ever more active as we let go of selfish and self-centred concerns, and our true nature emerges. In Northern Buddhism (see page 24), and particularly the Zen tradition, this is known as the *buddha*-nature.

The Triple Gem

The three principles of the Buddha, the Dharma (the Teachings) and the Sangha (the Community) is known as the Triple Gem. These three principles represent a living tradition in the here and now, and although we need to go back time and again to the teachings so as not to be led astray, what really matters is the practice right now, from moment to moment.

Life is made up of light and dark, joy and sorrow, success and failure; no matter who we are, no matter what our circumstances, all living beings must tread this way between birth and death. Life is short and we all must die. We are born with much inherent knowledge and wisdom; our folly

is that we know little of it and do not trust it. To become aware of this natural inbuilt wisdom, and to be able to trust in it at all times, is where Buddhist practices will lead.

Upon his enlightenment, the Buddha is said to have uttered these words:

> How wonderful, how miraculous, all beings, but all beings, are fully endowed with the wisdom and power of the Tathagata. But, sadly, human beings, due to sticky attachments, are not aware of it.

A person's inherent wisdom and power is hidden by his or her "sticky attachments" to the various fetters (see page 71). The wisdom and power of the Tathagata, however, is well able to deal with anything that life brings its way.

By extension, it is also possible to say that *buddha*-nature is equipped to deal with all the difficulties that life will bring. The way of practice is a cultivation of form that makes it possible for this inherent strength, resourcefulness, wisdom and natural compassion to emerge by the best means.

Don't Be Carried Away By Tears

There is a famous story told of the abbot of a Zen monastery, who, while out one day on his local walk, noticed a large crowd gathered at a funeral. He discovered he knew the family and joined the ceremony. Soon he was seen to be crying along with the rest of the congregation.

Later one of the locals approached him and said, "Master I saw you crying at the funeral. Surely you who are a great master are beyond this sort of thing?" [A reference to pleasure and pain.]

"No," he replied, "it is because of this that I am able to cry. To cry and not be carried away by tears, to laugh and not be carried away by laughter, is the way."

The crucial teaching contained in the anecdote is that the achievement is to live within the limits of the sensibilities and limitations of the human body, not trying to escape from experiencing life, but to live it without holding back.

Training the Heart

In Japan the Zen form of Buddhism attracted many samurai warriors and the story that follows encapsulates the changes that can occur through a training of the heart – no easy matter but one worth the effort.

A warrior had deserted his lord after a long inner struggle. He did so because he felt an overwhelming vocation for the Zen life. Having spent some twelve years in one of the monasteries in the mountains, he set out on pilgrimage. Before long he encountered a samurai on horseback who recognized him and made to strike him down but then decided against it as he was unwilling to sully his sword. Instead, he just spat in the monk's face as he rode by. In the simple act of wiping away the spittle, the monk realized in a flash what his reaction in former days would have been to such an insult. Deeply moved, he turned round to face the mountains where he had done his training, bowed, and composed a poem:

> The mountain is the mountain
> And the Way is the same as of old.
> Truly what has changed
> Is my own heart.

The samurai-turned-monk was no longer attached to the idea of defending his honour; he did not seek to fight back but simply wiped the spit from his face. This was a complete transformation of character, and it is one that only comes about with the cultivation of much reverence.

Growth stifled by attachment

When we plant a seed that grows into a flower or a tree it merely needs to grow into that – its form is already there. Cultivation of the heart is about removing the obstructions of attachment that prevent growth. The Lankavatara Sutra, first composed in the first century CE, speaks of the many external objects to which people get attached.

> Mahamati . . . the ignorant and simple minded, not knowing that the world is only something seen of the mind itself, cling to the multitudinousness of external objects, cling to the notion of being and non-being, oneness and otherness, bothness and not-bothness, existence and non-existence, eternity and non-eternity, and think they have a self nature of their own, all of which rises from the discriminations of the mind and is perpetuated by habit-energy, and from which they are given over to false imagination. It is all like a mirage in which springs of water are seen as if they were real. . . . In the same way, Mahamati, the ignorant and simple minded, their minds burning with the fires of greed, anger and folly [delusion], finding delight in the world of multitudinous forms, their thoughts obsessed with ideas of birth, growth and destruction, not well understanding what is meant by existent and non-existent, and being impressed by the erroneous discriminations and speculations, since beginningless time, fall into the habit of grasping this and that and thereby becoming attached to them.
>
> THE LANKAVATARA SUTRA

Mindfulness

> In mindfulness of body be well fixed,
> The monk restrained in the six spheres of sense,
> Ever composed, could his *nirvana* know.
>
> THE UDANA (IN THE KHUDDAKA NIKAYA)

The Sanskrit word *smrti*, or *sati* (P.), has been translated in many ways, including "awareness", "self-possession", "full consciousness" and "mindfulness". The practice of Buddhism is dependent on the cultivation of this ability. With it Buddhism is more than a mere intellectual system, it becomes a living path to "liberation" – the freedom from suffering that the Buddha speaks of in his teachings.

> Suppose the loveliest girl of the land was dancing and singing and a crowd assembled. A man was there wishing to live, not to die, wishing for happiness, averse to suffering. If someone said to him, "Good man, carry this bowl of oil filled to the brim between the crowd and the girl. A man with a sword will follow you, and if you spill even a drop he will cut off your head", would that man stop attending to that bowl of oil and turn his attention outward to the girl? This simile shows how you should train yourselves to direct awareness of the body.
>
> SAMYUTTA NIKAYA

Cultivating the body

The practice of mindfulness starts simply by cultivating the capacity to be alert to the body, most of the time, except during sleep. This process begins with the capability to be aware that we hear, see, sense, touch and taste and whether these are pleasant, unpleasant or neutral.

> You should not let your senses make a playground of your heart and mind.
>
> TIBETAN SAYING

Mindfulness progresses to include any emotional state of mind, culminating in the ability to see the workings of the mind, or mind-objects (*dhammanupassana*), and discern the complete nature of the mind and the heart. This means becoming fully aware of suffering, impermanence and the absence of any ultimate essence, or No-I (the "three signs of being", see page 62). It also entails recognition of the daily psychic reality of the "three fires" – desire, anger and delusion – and that an understanding of the laws of *karma*, the Four Noble Truths and the Noble Eightfold Path will lead to freedom. Mindfulness leads ultimately to the individual discovering what the Buddha himself discovered.

Human beings pride themselves on classifying tangible objects – animals have been classified into a kingdom, then divided and subdivided, resulting in groupings such as invertebrates, vertebrates, amphibians, reptiles, mammals, and so on. However, we do not do the same with the inner sphere; in fact, we are deficient in this, and remain largely ignorant of what goes on within. The cultivation of mindfulness is therefore extraordinarily important and was enshrined in the Satipatthana Sutta (see example, overleaf).

Discourse on Mindfulness

There is, monks, this one way to the purification of beings, for the overcoming of sorrow and distress, for the disappearance of pain and sadness, for the gaining of the right path, for the realization of *nirvana*: that is to say the four foundations of mindfulness.

What are the four? Here, monks, a monk abides contemplating body as body ardent, clearly aware and mindful, having put aside hankering and fretting for the world; he abides contemplating feelings as feelings . . . , he abides contemplating mind as mind . . .; he abides contemplating mind-objects as mind-objects, ardent, clearly aware and mindful, having put aside hankering and fretting for the world.

Again, *bhikkhu*s, when walking, a *bhikkhu* understands: "I am walking"; when standing, he understands: "I am standing"; when sitting, he understands: "I am sitting"; when lying down, he understands: "I am lying down"; or he understands accordingly, however his body is disposed.

In this way he abides contemplating the body as a body . . . both internally and externally . . . . And he abides independent, not clinging to anything in the world. That too is how a *bhikkhu* abides contemplating the body as a body.

The mindfulness of breathing

The Buddha's discourse then goes on to describe in great detail how we become aware of the body by becoming fully familiar with breathing, a process known as *anapanasati* – "being aware of the breath", or "mindfulness of breathing". This is a very simple exercise but one that, because of its simplicity, is undervalued and not cultivated enough:

> And how, monks, does a monk abide contemplating the body as body? Here a monk, having gone into the forest, or to the root of a tree, or to an empty place, sits down cross-legged, holding his body erect, having established mindfulness before him. Mindfully he breathes in, mindfully he breathes out. Breathing in a long breath, he knows that he breathes in a long breath, breathing out a long breath, he knows he breaths out a long breath. Breathing in a short breath, he knows that he breathes in a short breath, and breathing out a short breath, he knows that he breathes out a short breath. He trains himself, thinking: "I will breath out conscious of the whole body." He trains himself thinking: "I will breath out, conscious of the whole body." He trains himself thinking: "I will breathe in, calming the whole bodily process." He trains himself, thinking: "I will breathe out calming the whole bodily process."
>
> . . . So he abides contemplating the body as body internally, contemplating the body as body externally.

> . . . He abides contemplating arising phenomena in the body, he abides contemplating vanishing phenomena in the body, he abides contemplating both arising and vanishing phenomena in the body. Or else, mindfulness "that there is body" is present to him just to the extent necessary for knowledge and awareness.
>
> FROM THE SATIPATHHANA SUTTA
> (IN THE MAJJHIMA NIKAYA)

The human aggregates

The Buddha taught that a human being is a soul-less entity comprised of five components, or *skandhas* (*khandas*, P.): the physical body (*rupa*), feelings (*vendana*), perceptions (*samjna*), habitual mental dispositions (*samskara*) and consciousness (*vijnana*). Viewed in this way – the person as an aggregate or collection of components – all reality is a process. In a famous discourse about mental objects as a basis for meditation, the Buddha remarked:

> How, monks, does a monk live contemplating mental objects in the mental objects of the five aggregates of clinging?
>
> Herein, monks, a monk thinks: "Thus is material form; thus is the arising of material form; and thus is the disappearance of material form. Thus is feeling; thus is the arising of feeling; and thus is the disappearance of feeling. Thus is perception; thus is the arising of perception; and thus is the disappearance of perception. Thus are formations; thus is the arising of formations;

and thus is the disappearance of formations. Thus is consciousness; thus is the arising of consciousness; and thus is the disappearance of consciousness."

FROM THE MAHASUNNATA SUTTA
(IN THE MAJJHIMA NIKAYA)

To be mentally alert and attentive, to have ardour in pursuit of the objective, emerges increasingly as the practitioner perfects mindfulness. It is closely related to *bodhicitta*, the drive to enlightenment. The Buddha, on his deathbed, is said to have exhorted those around him "transient are all formations, strive on zealously (or heedfully)". Diligence is considered to be a foundation stone of progress, a sentiment expressed famously by the eight century CE Indian monk Shantideva:

> Just as all the footprints of living beings are surpassed by the footprint of the elephant, and the footprint of the elephant is considered as the mightiest among them, just so have all the meritorious qualities zeal as their foundation, and zeal is considered as the mightiest of these qualities.

FROM THE *BODHICARYAVATARA* BY SHANTIDEVA

True Supernatural Powers

Although mindfulness can confer considerable strength, in considering any such highly developed ability the real point can be missed. Insight alone will become just another road to pride and conceit. Within the Zen school there is a famous sermon on mastering supernatural powers:

> You say the Buddha has . . . six supernatural powers and that they are miraculous. But all the . . . demons have supernatural powers. Should they be Buddha? Followers of the Way, do not be deceived. . . .
>
> As I see it, all those . . . powers are karmic and dependent. They are not the . . . powers the Buddha possessed: Seeing without being deceived by colour and form; hearing without being deceived by sound; smelling without being deceived by smells; tasting without being deceived by tastes; touching without being deceived by touch; and thinking without being deceived by mental configurations. Therefore the six fields of form, sound, smell, taste, touch and mental configurations are all formless; they cannot bind the man of true independence.
>
> Although the . . . *skandha*s are leaky by nature, yet mastering them they become your supernatural powers here on earth.
>
> FROM THE *RECORD OF RINZAI* BY LINJI YIXUAN

The Smoking Anthill

Thus have I heard. On one occasion the Blessed One was living at Jeta's Grove while the venerable Kassapa was living at Blind Men's Grove. In the depth of the night a certain supernatural being, of beautiful appearance who illuminated the whole of the grove, approached Kassapa and stood at one side. The deity said to him: "*Bhikkhu, bhikkhu*, this anthill flames by day and fumes by night."

A *brahmin* spoke: "Dig in with the knife, wise one."

Digging with the knife, Kassapa came across a bar: "A bar, venerable sir."

The *brahmin* said: "Discard the bar and dig on, wise one."

Digging further, Kassapa came across a toad:
"A toad, venerable sir."

Thus spoke the *brahmin*: "Throw out the toad;
delve with the knife, you wise one."

Delving with the knife, the wise one saw a fork:
"A fork, venerable sir."

Thus spoke the *brahmin*: "Throw out the fork;
delve with the knife, you wise one."

Delving with the knife, the wise one saw a sieve:
"A sieve, venerable sir."

Thus spoke the *brahmin*: "Throw out the sieve;
delve with the knife, you wise one."

Delving with the knife, the wise one saw a
tortoise: "A tortoise, venerable sir."

Thus spoke the *brahmin*: "Throw out the tortoise;
delve with the knife, you wise one."

Delving with the knife, the wise one saw an axe
and a block: "An axe and a block, venerable sir."

Thus spoke the *brahmin*: "Throw out the axe and
block; delve with the knife, you wise one."

Delving with the knife, the wise one saw a piece
of meat: "A piece of meat, venerable sir."

Thus spoke the *brahmin*: "Throw out the piece of meat; delve with the knife, you wise one."

Delving with the knife, the wise one saw a Naga serpent: "A Naga serpent, venerable sir."

Thus spoke the *brahmin*: "Leave the Naga serpent; do not harm the Naga serpent; honour the Naga serpent."

"*Bhikkhu*, you should go to the Blessed One and ask him about this riddle. As the Blessed One tells you, so should you remember it. *Bhikkhu*, other than the Tathagata or a disciple of the Tathagata or one who has learned it from them, I see no one in this world with its gods, its Maras, and its Brahmas, in this generation with its recluses and *brahmin*s, its princes and its people, whose explanation of this riddle might satisfy the mind."

That is what was said by the deity, who thereupon vanished at once.

Then, when the night was over, the venerable Kassapa went to the Blessed One. After paying homage to him, he sat down at one side and told the Blessed One what had occurred. Then he asked:

Venerable sir, what is the anthill, what is the fuming by night, what is the flaming by day? Who is the brahmin, *who is the wise one? What is the knife, what is the delving, what is the bar, what is the toad, what is the fork, what is the sieve, what is the tortoise, what is the axe and block, what is the piece of meat, what is the Naga serpent?"*

Bhikkhu, the anthill is a symbol for this body, made of material form, consisting of the four great elements, procreated by a mother and father, built up out of boiled rice and porridge, and subject to impermanence, to being worn and rubbed away, to dissolution and disintegration.

What one thinks and ponders by night based upon one's actions during the day is the "fuming by night". The actions one undertakes during the day by body, speech, and mind after thinking and pondering by night is the "flaming by day".

The *brahmin* is a symbol for the Tathagata, accomplished and fully enlightened. The wise one is a symbol for a *bhikkhu* in higher training. The knife is a symbol for noble wisdom. The delving is a symbol for the arousing of energy.

The bar is a symbol for ignorance. "Throw out the bar: abandon ignorance. Delve with the knife, you wise one." This is the meaning.

The toad is a symbol for the despair due to anger. "Throw out the toad: abandon despair due to anger. Delve with the knife, you wise one." This is the meaning.

The fork is a symbol for doubt. "Throw out the fork: abandon doubt. Delve with the knife, you wise one." This is the meaning.

The sieve is a symbol for the five hindrances; namely, the hindrance of sensual desire, the hindrance of ill-will, the hindrance of sloth and torpor, the hindrance of restlessness and remorse, and the hindrance of doubt. "Throw out the sieve: abandon the five hindrances. Delve with the knife, you wise one." This is the meaning.

The tortoise is a symbol for the five aggregates affected by clinging; namely, the material form aggregate affected by clinging, the feeling aggregate affected by clinging, the perception aggregate affected by clinging, the formations aggregate affected by clinging, and the consciousness aggregate affected by clinging. "Throw out the tortoise: abandon the five aggregates affected by clinging. Delve with the knife, you wise one." This is the meaning.

The axe and the block is a symbol for the five cords of sensual pleasure – forms identifiable by the eye that are wished for, desired, agreeable, and likeable, connected with sensual desire, and provocative of lust; sounds identifiable by the ear . . . odours identifiable by the nose . . . flavours identifiable by the tongue . . . tangibles identifiable by the body that are wished for, desired, agreeable, and likeable, connected with sensual desire, and provocative of lust. "Throw out the axe and the block: abandon the five cords of sensual pleasure. Delve with the knife, you wise one." This is the meaning.

The piece of meat is a symbol for delight and lust. "Throw out the piece of meat: abandon delight and lust. Delve with the knife, you wise one." This is the meaning.

The Naga serpent is a symbol for a *bhikkhu* who has destroyed the taints. "Leave the Naga serpent; do not harm the Naga serpent; honour the Naga serpent." This is the meaning.

THE PARABLE OF THE ANTHILL, FROM THE VAMMIKA SUTTA, IN THE MAJJHIMA NIKAYA

Meditation

The word for "meditation" doesn't actually exist in Pali or Sanskrit, neither is there a word to describe the practices of mental development. The words that are found include *bhavana* – which means cultivation, or to bring into existence – and *citta*, or the cultivation of mind. *Citta* means the spiritual and emotional centre of a person – their "heart" in the sense of being whole-hearted, or having one's heart in something. These terms are used in other spiritual systems, probably because they refer to natural states of being – and as such states are natural they can be cultivated until they become, more or less, permanent.

Every school of Buddhism recognizes three stages to this cultivation, which is reflected in the three categories the Noble Eightfold Path is organized into (see page 106). The first is the cultivation of moral discipline, the second is the development of concentrated absorption, the third is the attainment of wisdom. *Bhavana* is thus the cultivation of the heart and consciousness (or mind), relating to composure, concentration, and meditation, which culminates in higher wisdom and spiritual emancipation.

Insight and concentration

The practices that have become known in the West as "meditation" have two aspects to them: insight (*vipasanna*) and concentration (*samadhi*). By calming (*samatha*), that is quieting overactive thought-streams, insight will naturally arise, which in turn develops into awareness. The process is not mysterious – when "the heat of the moment" has dissipated and we are calm again we see things much more clearly. This "clear-seeing", or insight, is *vipasanna*.

Many individuals have spent a long time in their agitated state, so to calm down their whole system gradually can take years of practice. The real insight, of course, is into the insubstantiality and impermanence of all existence, but there are many "lesser" insights on the way that contribute to an increasing sense of freedom and engender a warmth of heart. As the journey along the path progresses, we become calmer, we gain deeper insight, and we gradually become kinder and friendlier.

Concentration (*samadhi*), or absorption, is about becoming "at-one-with" what we are doing. Again, this is a simple matter and we do it much of the time, especially when we are interested in and enjoying something. Through spiritual practice of *samadhi* – often undertaken in a formal, cross-legged, seated posture – we can become immersed in the most unappealing tasks and subjects. It provides one of the best ways to still a wandering mind. A classic tale from the Pali canon, "The Monkey" (opposite), reveals that the practice rests on the development of awareness. Another traditional tale, "The Samadhi Deer" (see pages 166–167), illustrates the importance of the part played by the practice of "counting the breath" in helping us to become familiar with the nature of mind – because as we struggle to sit still the thought processes seem to become more and more active. Humans have a tendency to become self-conscious: watching ourselves rather than forgetting ourselves.

The Monkey

*Bhikkhu*s, there are rugged areas in the Himalayas, the king of mountains, where neither monkeys nor human are found. There are rugged areas where monkeys are found but not humans. There are delightful, more accessible regions where both monkeys and humans are found – and there hunters set out traps of sticky pitch along the monkey trails to catch monkeys.

When they see the pitch, those monkeys who are not foolish or impetuous by nature avoid it warily. But a monkey who is foolish and impetuous by nature approaches the pitch, seizes it with its paw and gets stuck. Thinking, "I will free my paw", it grabs the stuck paw with the free paw and gets stuck. Thinking, "I will free both paws", it uses a foot and gets caught there. Thinking, "I will free both paws and my foot", it uses the other foot and gets caught there. Thinking, "I will free both paws and feet", it applies its mouth and gets caught there.

Thus, *bhikkhu*s, the monkey, trapped in five ways, lies there whimpering. It has met with disaster and the hunter can do with it as he pleases. The hunter spears it, fastens it to a block of wood and goes off where he wants. So it is, *bhikkhu*s, when one strays outside one's domain into that of others.

MEDITATION

Therefore, *bhikkhu*s, do not stray outside your own domain and into that of others. Mara will spot an opportunity among those who stray outside their own domain into that of others, and Mara will get a hold on them.

For a *bhikkhu*, what is not his proper domain? It is the five strands of sensual pleasure: the forms recognizable to the eye, the sounds recognizable to the ear, the smells recognizable to the nose, the flavours recognizable to the tongue, the tactile sensations recognizable to the body. For a *bhikkhu*, these are not his proper domain.

Move, *bhikkhu*s, within what is your proper domain, your own ancestral area. In one who moves within his own proper domain, his own ancestral area, Mara will not gain an opening, will not get a hold.

And what is a *bhikkhu*'s own proper domain, his own ancestral area? It is the four kinds of mindfulness. What four? Here, *bhikkhu*s, a *bhikkhu* dwells contemplating the body in the body – ardent, clearly comprehending, mindful, having removed covetousness and displeasure in regard to the world. He dwells contemplating feelings in feelings . . . mind in mind . . . phenomena in phenomena, ardent, clearly comprehending, mindful, having removed covetousness and displeasure in regard to the world. This is a *bhikkhu*'s proper domain, his own ancestral area.

FROM THE MAKKATA SUTTA (SAMYUTTA NIKAYA)

The Samadhi Deer

Once there was a simple woodsman who lived in a forest and every day he would collect wood for the king's palace. One day he was in a clearing in the forest cutting wood when he noticed a most beautiful deer standing quite still, not far from him. Quite enthralled, he put down his axe and, looking at the deer, he thought, "What a beautiful animal". At that moment the deer spoke and it said, "What a beautiful animal". The woodsman was taken aback and said to himself, "Did I hear right?" – and the deer, looking at him, said, "Did I hear right?" Now completely taken aback, he said to himself, "Can it be true, a talking deer?" At which the deer replied, "Yes, and now you're thinking 'Can it be true a talking deer?'" The woodsman looked away and he thought, "It can probably lip-read" – and the deer said, "Now you're thinking that I can probably lip read".

Really taken aback now, he thought, "If I can catch this talking, mind-reading deer the king

will richly reward me". To his horror the deer
said, "Now you think if you can catch this talking,
mind-reading deer and bring me to the king,
he will richly reward you". At that point the
woodsman sprung towards the deer, at which
point the deer, knowing exactly what he was
going to do, had already anticipated him and
sprung back. And so it went on for quite a time,
and whatever the woodsman thought or did, the
deer repeated or anticipated. Finally, enraged, and
in desperation the woodsman set about chopping
the wood with ferocity, accompanied by the deer
saying, "It's no good you know, whatever you
do, I can still read your mind". So he chopped
harder and harder to the accompaniment of
the commentary of the deer. As he chopped
and chopped the voice seemed to fade, and
then suddenly with one last supreme effort he
drove the axe with complete, single-minded
concentration at the log – at that very moment
the axehead flew off and struck the deer in the
middle of the head, and the mind-reading, talking
deer fell to the ground unconscious.

States of consciousness

Samadhi has numerous states or levels, increasingly subtle and refined as the overactive consciousness settles down. The Buddha described it as water that clears if it is left to settle, gradually becoming clearer and clearer.

> Then, Lord, is it for the sake of realizing the practice of contemplation that the brethren live the holy life under the Exalted One?
>
> No, indeed, Mahali. It is not for the sake of this that the brethren live the holy life under my guidance. There are other higher and more excellent things, Mahali, for the realization of which the brethren live the holy life under my guidance.
>
> FROM THE BRAHMAJALA SUTTA (DIGHA NIKAYA)

The first level is one of detachment from sensuality and it is accompanied by rapture and joy. The second level is when thoughts and thinking subside, and, born from concentration, *samadhi* becomes filled with rapture and joy. The third level of absorption is marked by equanimity and alertness. The fourth level is marked by the absence of pleasure and pain, and even joy and grief; there is an increased and refined equanimity and a lucid awareness, or mindfulness (*smrti* S., *sati*, P.).

The next four levels of consciousness represent the spheres of infinite space, infinite consciousness, and infinite nothingness, until finally the practitioner reaches the sphere of neither perception nor non-perception. But even these states are impermanent. The attainment of these *dhayanas* (*jhanas*, P., often used to mean meditation) is not an end in itself, but simply a means to becoming humble. Indeed, the Theravedan Brahmajala Sutta (*brahma* means "perfect wisdom" and *jala* "all-embracing-net-of-views"), the first *sutta* in the Digha Nikaya, makes it clear that a belief in any of these states as an end in itself is a false view.

> By passing quite beyond the plain of nothingness, the monk enters into and abides in the plane of neither-perception-nor-non-perception. By passing quite beyond this plane, he enters into and abides in the ceasing of feeling and perceiving. He has now crossed over the entanglement in the world and is one who, as in the case of mastery in the four *dhyana*s and the remaining four planes, has made Mara blind and, blotting out his vision so that it has no range, goes unseen by the malign one.
>
> MAJJHIMA NIKAYA

Although the *dhayanas* map out the regions of consciousness, enlightenment comes only when we see the world with the same absolute clarity as the Buddha, when we perceive the world as the Buddha perceived it, and become "awake". In the meantime, the practice of meditation greatly enhances the perception of reality. As the Pali canon puts it:

> With his heart thus serene, made pure, translucent, cultured, void of evil, supple, ready to act, firm and imperturbable, he directs and bends down his mind to the knowledge of

the memory of his previous temporary states. He
recalls to his mind . . . one birth, or two or three
. . . or a thousand or a hundred thousand births,
through many an eon of dissolution, many an eon
of both dissolution and evolution.

FROM THE SAMANNAPHALA SUTTA

(DIGHA NIKAYA)

Wisdom

Ultimately, the practitioner "disappears in the trackless" in the manner of an explorer journeying on, deeper and deeper into the indescribable, yet on this journey the traveller is increasingly more at home in an ephemeral and fleeting world. Having given up all attempts at trying to be someone, and becoming what is ultimately the true mystery of the human condition – *buddha*-nature; expressing it and celebrating it in all things, he realizes the goal of the practice.

> Whoever has attained faith and wisdom,
> His state of mind, well harnessed, leads him on.
> With Conscience as its shaft, Mind its yoke and
> Heedfulness the watchful charioteer:
> The furnishings of righteousness, the Car;
> Rapture the axle; Energy the wheels; and
> Calm, yoke-fellow of the balanced mind.
> Desirelessness their drapery:
> Goodwill and Harmlessness are his weapons,
> Together with detachment of the mind.
> Endurance is the armour,
> And to attain the peace, that Car rolls on.
> It is built by self, by one's own self become this

Chariot, incomparable, supreme:
Seated in it the sages leave the world,
And assuredly they win the victory.

DIGHA NIKAYA

Index

Abhidamma Pitaka 26
Abhidarmakosa 128, 131
action, willed *see* karma
Aditta Sutta 87
anatman see No-I
annica see impermanence
Anattalakkhana Sutta 72
Anguttara Nikaya 57, 65, 67, 70, 81, 82, 96, 105, 114
"Anthill, Parable of the" 150–157
asceticism 21, 92
attachment 15, 64, 102, 138
avidya see ignorance
Avatamsaka Sutra 48, 119
awareness 15, 45

Bodhicaryavatara 120, 149
bodhisattva 25, 128, 129, 130
bodhi-tree 42
Brahmajala Sutta 168
brahma-vihara 121, 131
breathing 146
Buddha, the
  birth 18–19
  childhood 19
  death 24
  scriptural sources 24–30
    see also individual titles of texts
  teachings, spread of 30–36
  wanderings 10–11, 19–22
buddha-nature 78, 132, 134
Buddhaghosa 60, 67, 132
"Burning House, Parable of the" 38

compassion 64
concentration 106, 110, 160, 162
consciousness 21, 168–170
cosmogeny 50–51
craving 45, 53, 59, 60, 78, 79, 80, 81, 88, 92, 96, 101–102, 119, 138
  see also Fire Sermon, the

death 74–75
delusion 47, 62, 82, 93
  see also Fire Sermon, the
desire *see* craving
Dhammacakkappavattana Sutta 90

Dhammapada, the
  "Anger" 80
  "Impurity" 79, 81
  "Old Age" 65
  "On Earnestnes" 118
  "Punishment" 81
  "The Bhikkhu" 121
  "The Brahmana" 79, 93, 94, 116, 117, 119
  "The Buddha" 60
  "The Thousands" 75, 112
  "The Way" 82
  "The Wise Man" 111
  "The World" 60
  "Thirst" 79, 80, 81
  "Twin Verses" 55, 58
dharma (element) 49, 129, 130
Dharma, the (Law) 16, 23, 42, 49, 64, 67, 73, 81, 93
dhyanas see consciousness
Diamond Sutra 27, 65, 71
Digha Nikaya 109, 168, 170, 171
dukkha see suffering

enlightenment 10, 22, 60, 70, 90, 134, 149
equanimity 121

fetters 44, 117
Fire Sermon, the 84–87
First Sermon, the 98–99, 106–108
  see also Four Noble Truths
five aggregates 67, 147
five precepts 116
Flower Garland Sutra 48, 119
Four Noble Truths 96–105
four vows 128

giving 114–115
greed 79, 81, 82, 138

hatred 79, 80, 81, 82, 92, 117, 138
  see also Fire Sermon, the
Heart Sutra 27, 119
Hsin Hsin Ming 93, 95, 120

ignorance 44, 55, 59, 88, 123, 138
impermanence 23, 47, 62, 65, 66–67, 69
"It Will Pass", story of 68–69

Kalama Sutta 104, 105
karma 44, 52, 54–55, 57, 58, 79, 82
Khuddaka Nikaya 44, 51, 53, 54, 59, 75, 121, 140
"Kisa Gotami", story of 74–75
kleshas see three fires

Lakkhana Sutta 65
Lankavatara Sutra 138
livelihood 109
"Log, Parable of the" 124–127
Lotus Sutra 29, 38
loving-kindness 82, 114, 120–121

Madhyamika school 92
Mahasunnata Sutta 148
Mahayana tradition 24, 25, 26–27
Majjhima Nikaya 121, 144, 147, 148, 157, 169
Makkata Sutta 165
meditation 21, 121, 160–171
Middle Path, the 90–95
mindfulness 109, 140–157
"Monkey", story of the 163–165
morality 106, 114, 116–117
Mumonkan 83

nidanas see fetters
nirvana 10, 47, 62, 71, 75, 94, 119
Noble Eightfold Path 90, 91, 96, 99, 106–113
No-I 47, 62, 71–73

paramitas 114–131
"Path to Purity" see *Visuddhimagga*
patience 117
perfections *see paramitas*

rebirth 10, 44, 52–53, 57, 59, 96, 120
Record of Rinzai 150
renunciation 119
resolution 120

samadhi see concentration
"Samadhi Deer", story of the 166–167
Samannaphala Sutta 170
samsara see rebirth
Samyutta Nikaya 72, 75, 87, 91, 99, 117, 127, 140, 165

Sarvastivada school 128
Satipatthana Sutta 143, 144, 147
Shantideva 119, 120, 149
Shobogenzo 73
shunyata 52
skandhas 150 *see also* five aggregates
suffering 13, 36, 42, 44, 47, 51, 53, 60, 62, 65, 66, 70, 96, 97, 99
Sutta Nipata 51, 53, 59
Sutta Pitaka 26, 42, 128
Suzuki, Daisetz Teitaro 83

Tathagata 10, 51, 134
ten fetters 71
texts *see under* individual titles
Theravada tradition 24
Therigatha 75
thought, independence of 104–105
three fires 47, 52, 78–89
three signs of being 47, 62–75, 78, 101
Tibetan canon 29–30
Tipitaka 25–26
trilaksana see three signs of being
Triple Gem 67, 132
trsna see craving
truthfulness 120
Turning of the Wheel, the 90

Udana 44, 54, 121, 140

Vajrayana school 35
Vasubandhu 128
vigour 118
Vinaya Pataka 25
virtue *see paramitas*
Visuddhimagga 60, 66

Wheel of Life, the 52–53
wisdom 64, 70, 82, 106, 114, 118–119, 170

Yammika Sutta 157
Yogachara school 92, 128

zeal 149 *see also* vigour
Zen 8, 13, 32, 65, 67, 73, 83, 93, 95, 132, 136, 137, 150
Zenrinkushu 65, 67

Further reading

Bechert, Heinz and Gombrich, Richard. (eds.) *The World of Buddhism*. Thames and Hudson: London, 1984.
Biddulph, Desmond. *1001 Pearls of Buddhist Wisdom*. Duncan Baird Publishers: London: 2006.
Carus, Paul. *The Gospel of Buddha*. The Open Court Publishing Co: Chicago, 1904.
Eckel, Malcolm David. *Understanding Buddhism*. Duncan Baird Publishers: London: 2003.
Max Muller, F. (trans.) *The Dhammapada: The Essential Teachings of the Buddha*. Watkins Publishing: London, 2006.
Oldenberg, Hermann. *Buddha: His Life, His Doctrine, His Order*. Williams and Norgate: London, 1882.
Suzuki, D.T. *The Essence of Buddhism*. The Buddhist Society: London, 1947.
Trainor, Kevin. (ed.) *Buddhism*. Duncan Baird Publishers: London: 2004.

About the authors

Dr. Desmond Biddulph is vice president and chairman of The Buddhist Society. He is editor of *The Middle Way*, the journal of The Buddhist Society, and author of *1001 Pearls of Buddhist Wisdom* (DBP). He is a Jungian therapist with a practice in London, and he has written many articles on Buddhism and psychology.

Darcy Flynn has been a student of Buddhism for many years and has travelled throughout India and China. She has a theatre and film company in London and has directed an international film festival.

About the photographer

John Cleare is an internationally renowned photographer specializing in mountains and landscapes. His photographs illustrate *Tales from the Tao*, *Classic Haiku* (both DBP) and an edition of the *Tao Te Ching* (Watkins Publishing).